Hamster to Harmony

Get off the 'wheel' and live your best life!

Maurice DeCastro

Hamster to Harmony First published in 2009 by;

Ecademy Press

6, Woodland Rise, Penryn, Cornwall, UK. TR10 8QD

info@ecademy-press.com

www.ecademy-press.com

Printed and Bound by; Lightning Source in the UK and USA

Set in Warnock and Helveica Neue by Charlotte Mouncey

Printed on acid-free paper from managed forests. This book is printed on demand, so no copies will be remaindered or pulped.

ISBN 978-1-905823-48-2

For Reece

CONTENTS

Chapter 1

Guidance from a hamster

"Happiness is when what you think, what you say, and what you do are in harmony."

Mahatma Gandhi

When I was a young boy of maybe 5 or 6 years old, I remember asking myself and anyone who would listen to me the same question over and over again. The question was this: 'How do some people get to be so lucky?' You see, it was my perception as a small boy that my family wasn't very lucky and that luck was something that only belonged to other people. In fact, at the time, it seemed like luck was this thing that belonged to everyone else, everyone except us. It wasn't horrendous; we weren't abused, mistreated, sick, homeless, disabled or suffered in any way. It just seemed to me at the time that everyone had much more than we did.

I guess to me as a 5-year-old life was all about having things and we didn't seem to have very much compared to everyone else. I would wonder how all of my friends and neighbours seemed to have so much more and how they got to be so lucky.

I was one of six children growing up with two very loving parents who just didn't seem to have much money. In fact they didn't seem to have any money. My father worked, while my mother did her best to look after the six of us.

My father drank way too much, spending most of his hard-earned wages on alcohol. Not only did this mean that there was even less money for such a large household, but the effects of the alcohol often left him emotionally and mentally distant from the family. He was a good man with a kind and loving heart, it was just that his only real friend was alcohol. I guess like any good friend, that's who he chose to spend most of his time with. At such a young age I could never quite understand why all my father ever seemed to do was just go to work, come home and sleep. While he pursued this routine my mother spent most of her time, as did all six children as we grew older, answering the phone to debt collectors.

I would wonder why I always had to walk two miles to get to school while all of my friends were driven to school by their parents. I wondered why my school uniform was always old, tatty and worn out because my two older brothers had worn the same uniform for years before me. I would wonder why all of my friends had the best toys, games and training shoes, when I had to settle for what seemed at the time like much less. I wondered why my friends were going on holiday to Spain and even Disney World when the furthest we got to was the local park.

At its very worst I would wonder why I would come home from school so often to find my mother crying as she frantically searched behind the sofa to see if she could find some loose change to be able to buy food for the six of us. I'd even wonder why my father came home from work so often drunk and why he and my mother argued as he went to bed to sleep off the alcohol, before waking up to start drinking again.

None of it seemed to make sense to me as a small boy growing up. 'How do some people get to be so lucky?' I would ask myself over and over again.

So I left school at the earliest possible opportunity aged 16 to go and earn some money so I could put many of these injustices right. I made a decision the day I left to go and find the answer to the question that I had been asking for the last 10 years of my very young life. I began by reading in the library; I read autobiographies, personal development books and anything that gave the slightest hint that it may contain the answer.

Well, it didn't take me long at all to realise that for those 10 long years I had been asking the wrong question. The questions should never have been, 'How do some people get to be so lucky?' The question I should have been asking all of those years was, 'What does it take to be successful?'

You see, I started to learn that when I looked around me and saw all of these other people with these wonderful things and leading much more interesting lives than my family, that it wasn't down to luck. What I learned was that most of those people had created better lives through the way they thought and behaved. Whilst there was often an element of luck involved, most of their 'success' was entirely down to them. I began to learn that what I needed to do was to study success.

So I started to do exactly that; I studied success. I went back to the library, started buying books on how to be successful and as I saved up enough money I would go to seminars and buy tapes and video programmes. I did everything I could to learn how one day I could be in a position to take my children to Disney World and drive them to school and to make sure that each year at the start of term they always had a brand new school uniform.

The more I learned, the more I applied and I found that many of the ideas either didn't really work or just weren't right for me. There were, however, a lot of very sound ideas which seemed to take me on a more lucrative path. But that was part of the problem for me, as I had defined success as a 5-year-old, as having things, as having money; the good news was it worked to a degree as I achieved my goal. When my son was 5 years old I had the money to take him to Disney World, my wife and I drove him to school every day and he always, always had a brand new school uniform at the start of term.

Somehow though, at some point, it still wasn't enough. There was something missing. I became a grown man with a beautiful wife, a young son and I was working long hours whilst hating my job. I was overweight, overstressed, drinking too much, suffering from anxiety and overall not the nicest person in the world to be with.

I finally realised that it had taken me many more years to work out that I had been asking the wrong question yet again. Even though I had changed the question, it was still the wrong one. The question should never have been, 'What does it take to be lucky or successful?' The real question I should have been asking and studying was, 'What does it take to be fulfilled?' Or at the very least I should have defined success as fulfilment.

My definition of fulfilment was, and still is, to just be me, the real me, and enjoy health, wealth, peace and happiness. For me it's about harmony across every area of my life.

As difficult and as insane as it may be to believe and accept, it was a hamster who finally taught me the art of fulfilment and harmony. Everything that I had learned and studied over so many years finally all fell into place. Fifteen huge pieces of the jigsaw of life all put into place by a hamster... These chapters represent those pieces.

The hamster's name was Botley; well, at least that was the way my 5-year-old son pronounced it. The hamster's real name, at the point of his adoption, was Mutley (named after Dick Dastardly's dog on the cartoon show *Wacky Races*, for those of you old enough to remember) but like most 5-year-olds, pronunciation isn't always their greatest strength, so we very early on settled for Botley. You see, Botley belonged to my son Reece, who loved this marathon-running fur ball with all of his heart and soul, yet couldn't quite get his name right. I don't think it ever really mattered very much to Botley though, because his sole interest in life was keeping me awake at night, or at least it seemed that way for some considerable time. You could just as easily have called him Rudolph for all he cared.

Botley was the proud resident of a small, but highly equipped cage, on the Formica work surface of our kitchen. He was just a few short inches long but as wide as a bus with cheeks the same colour as a number three to Crystal Palace. He had all of the latest hamster gadgetry known to man let alone a small beast. It's only now when I look back that it occurs to me that, at the age of 5, my son must have been exposed to a lot of old Bond movies, as Botley's cage was fitted out as though he was the 007 of hamsters. It's probably a good job he wasn't the hamster with the golden gun, because I may well have found that quite useful during his 3am spinning episodes.

Despite having everything a hamster could possibly want, Botley made it perfectly clear that he wasn't interested in any of it; in fact his only interest, care and indeed every thought in the entire universe, was for his wheel. This never ceased to intrigue me: how could such a clinically obese hamster, who clearly appeared to suffer from high blood pressure (as evident from his scarlet-red cheeks), maintain the physique he did when his every waking second revolved around running? Where to, what from, what for, nobody, but nobody knew.

I often wondered whether maybe it was just his genetic make up, or perhaps a hormone problem. Who knows with hamsters, eh? Botley lived to run. He never slept, he never stopped (not even to eat), in fact whilst there was never a shortage of Botley droppings in his cage we never, ever saw him pause for a moment to relieve himself. This hamster was a marvel of the modern animal world, so much so I even considered opening him up to scientific study a short while before he left us to journey to hamster heaven.

For a short time I became obsessed with Botley's behaviour. This was largely driven by my paranoia as I had totally and utterly convinced myself that Botley's purpose on this planet was to keep me awake at night. After all, I rationalised to myself, if we humans have a purpose (even though most of us spend our whole lives trying to work out what it is), then why shouldn't the same go for hamsters? What I just couldn't seem to work out was why Botley would make it his life's purpose to persecute me.

Night, after night, after night, after night I lay awake in my bed driven to despair by the spinning of the dreaded wheel. In fact, at its peak during the course of one evening I counted 64,324 spins! I'd convinced myself that if counting sheep had therapeutic sleep-inducing properties, then this must get close. I was very, very wrong; it didn't, ever!

It got so bad I was driven to desperate action, ranging from the obvious of stuffing cotton wool in my ears, locking Botley in the downstairs lavatory, sabotaging his wheel, putting rubber thimble-like things on his feet, and spending several hours in the middle of the night working out just why on earth it was that this Olympian athlete of a hamster (in stamina, not appearance) chose to ruin my life in this way. Why, why, why would it never stop running? Why did it start in the first place? Where on earth did it think it was going and would it ever realise it was never getting anywhere?

What I found even stranger than this was why I was the only one who was troubled by the spinning and kept awake all night. Both my wife and son were totally oblivious to Botley's racket. I very quickly became a nocturnal expert on hamsters, although I also realised that it was never to count for very much because Botley would just continue to run.

During the course of my research I even read somewhere that hamsters are known to run up to 15 miles during the course of just one night. I never did establish exactly why such distances were necessary; after all, I knew it wasn't for them to lose weight, or to look good, get fit, participate in marathons or the Olympics, and I knew it certainly wasn't because they were being followed around by Dr Gillian McKeith the famous author and star of the television programme *You Are What You Eat* bravely tackling the UK's growing hamster obesity dilemma. I was certain that the country did not have a hamster obesity problem. I knew it wasn't a self image issue either as you don't see too many hamster weight watchers clubs or hamster makeover programmes around. Besides he always seemed the happiest member of the family.

I learned to my devastation and mental torture that hamsters simply liked to run for fun! I also read many reports warning that hamsters should not actually run too much because they can become exhausted and dehydrated. So it seemed to me that the only real way to get Botley to stop running was to teach him to read. Yet I stood more chance of becoming Queen! Slowly but surely I began to resign myself to the fact that my life was to be dominated by a spinning hamster wheel and I had a choice: I could complain and continue to upset myself with it, or I could accept it and get on with the rest of my life. After all, this had already gone far too far.

What I didn't realise, at that time, was that somehow subconsciously this sad obsession with Botley was to trigger a change in my life which would have a dramatic impact on me and my family forever. This didn't become clear until shortly after Botley's death (which incidentally I am certain my wife believes to this day had something to do with me, although I swear I never touched him. Yes, the thought had occurred to me once or twice, but for all my faults, not even I could stoop so low).

One morning, the following week, I found myself driving the same route to the same office that I had been driving to every morning for the last 16 years, but this morning was to be different. Very different! As I drove toward the seven-storey glass front of the insurance building I worked in, I got caught up in traffic for a few minutes just a few yards from the car park. Normally, I would puff and blow and rant and rave in the usual manner cursing the design of the road, the other drivers, the car park, the government and life in general. Today though was different, in fact I don't ever recall a time when I felt calmer, more relaxed or focused. It was like I had entered some kind of parallel universe where time stood still. At the time it seemed as though I was stuck for an eternity as I could see the very staircase I had walked up every morning at the same time every day for 16 years.

I had nowhere else to go, nothing to do whilst stuck in the car and it wasn't the first time I was held up like that in the same position. In fact I couldn't even begin to count how many times I had been caught up in traffic, in almost that very same spot so many times before, yet for some reason this time was to be different. Strangely, it was almost as though I had miraculously acquired telescopic vision and 'bionic' hearing. I could see right through the slightly tinted sky-blue glass to see and hear colleagues and friends that I had worked with for so many years make their way slowly up the staircase where they were to spend anything up to the next 12 hours doing the very same thing they had done every day for so many years, in the same place, in the same way, in the same environment, with the same people, for the same pay, with largely the same results.

I could see their painful climb, and solemn, tired expressions. It was as though I could even tune into the conversations they were having with each other as they crawled to their desks. I remember the movie *Groundhog Day* springing to mind. Though this wasn't Hollywood, it was very real and most definitely wasn't comedy. Up until that moment I had always believed that I was quite happy with my life. After all, I had a good job, a roof over my head, a beautiful wife and son and even though there was always too much month at the end of the money we still managed to eat and go on holiday every now and then.

As far as the company and the job were concerned I knew both inside out and even thought I would retire there some day. My hairline had already seemed to have taken early re-tirement, so I figured the rest of me would naturally decline there too.

This was no ordinary traffic jam; somehow I had entered a moment of truth, my moment of truth, thanks to my old pal Botley. It seemed that despite all of my bitterness and resent-ment towards this hamster during his brief life on this earth, he was up there in hamster heaven prompting me to stand back for a moment and take stock of my life. It wasn't just about my job; he made me stop to think about my entire life. The question for me was whether this was his way of haunting and punishing me, or his way of offering divine guidance. I realised it could have been much worse: he could have just locked me in the lavatory as I had so often done to him. I sat there still and silently for what seemed like a lifetime, staring at people I had known for most of my working life, yet somehow, all I could really see was Botley, spinning aimlessly and endlessly in his wheel.

Of course it didn't take me very long to realise that even though I was sitting comfortably in my car, Botley was showing me myself on that treadmill. It was me on the wheel and I was spinning out of control. Of course it was metaphorical, but it seemed as real as anything; the staircase was the hamster wheel, my wheel, and I was just about to run my 15 miles again. The same 15 miles I had run every day for 16 years.

I had forgotten to give my life that much thought up to that point; I just got on with it living on autopilot. Nothing ever changed; everywhere I went everyone I knew, including me, was still complaining about too much month at the end of the money, moaning about the company, groaning about the politics, whinging about the changes and longing desperately for the good old days. Of course we smiled, had group hugs, and got as drunk as we could at Christmas parties, but where was it all heading? We pretended to love and care for one another, that is at least until performance dropped somewhere in the organisation and everyone put their head in the sand after looking to elicit blame with fingers pointing everywhere.

What was our real purpose, our real contribution? What was the emotional, mental, physical and even spiritual payback for expending all of that energy, all of that time, loyalty and commitment? Where would it all end? What was to happen to me? Was I a victim of life just handling whatever seemed to happen to me or was I in control? Was it really me creating my life?

It suddenly dawned on me that some of us, including me at the time, were no different from Botley. We were running hard on our own treadmill. The critical difference was, we didn't have to. We, unlike Botley (who was programmed to live his life on the wheel), had a choice. I was soon to realise that we had so much choice. I already knew this of course, as I found this out when I set about finding out 'how to be lucky' and 'how to be successful' when leaving school. The trouble was I knew it but I didn't really understand it up to that point and what I knew I seemed to have forgotten anyway. In fact, what was ironic was that not only did it appear to me that we were behaving the same as my old friend Botley, but we also (or at least some of us) were starting to look the same (of course with a lot less hair), that is, out of shape physically despite all of that expended energy, and many of us also had the red cheeks from elevated blood pressure.

I knew that Botley was trying to tell me something; I realised and believed that I and many of my colleagues were 'sleep-walking' our way through life. We could never have been described as truly conscious and totally responsible for our own lives, because how many of us could put our hands on our hearts and say we were energised, excited, fulfilled or even, at the very least, just really happy with the path we were on and where we were heading? In fact, I'm not even convinced that any of us really even knew where we were heading.

We were paying the bills, had roofs over our heads and food in our stomachs, but we were all still buying lottery tickets and living in a world where we had convinced ourselves that life would get better once something else happened to us first, for which we were actually taking no responsibility or action over. We would be ok once we got that promotion, won the lottery, lost weight, gave up smoking, got the attention and love we craved, got the new car, bigger house, better relationship, more sex, flat screen TV, holiday, more money that we needed, etc, etc, etc.

Even though I was only stuck in that car for a few short minutes I faced the huge disturbing reality and opportunity of seeing my life the way it really was. Little had I realised just how much Botley and I had in common. Who would have thought it, me and my son's hamster...the same!

I was married to the most gorgeous woman, who gave me the most precious gift of my life, a beautiful son, and I was on autopilot, working in a job I no longer really liked; I had just stopped growing and started stagnating. I had lost my passion, energy, enthusiasm and excitement and really was living to pay the bills, which with a young son was now more important than ever. I was living in fear, overweight, drinking too much, suffering from anxiety and stressed out of my eyeballs. All of my focus was on survival and just getting through the day. I had lost all concept of self worth, to be a good husband, a good father and even just a good person who loved life. My focus had been on success and success to me, up until that time, was about being able to pay the bills and have things.

The toughest realisation of all though, was that I had entangled myself in my very own self-created web. I had worked hard and diligently all of my life and found myself in a position which had taken all of my energy and confidence. It even got to the point where I had just convinced myself I could never get a job anywhere else and that this was my life...forever. Ironically, all of my effort, all of my energy and drive which had led me to what I had regarded, up until that point, as success had turned against me without me even realising it. I was trapped, under-stimulated and very bored. Yet it seemed that everyone, including me, was oblivious to what was going on around me; everyone that is except Botley. I had simply stopped growing and this hamster knew it; despite all of my bad feelings towards him, he was here to help me. It was only in that moment that I understood the true difference between Botley and me. The difference was that I was more than a creature of my environment and habit: I had the benefit of choice. I could get off the wheel; I could do or be whatever I wanted to do or be. I could have whatever I wanted. For Botley the scenery never ever changed. I could change my scenery at any time to any thing.

All I needed to do was wake up. It wasn't just about work. Botley was showing me that everything was out of control. I was bored, unfulfilled and under-stimulated at work, not getting any further after 16 years. I was also spinning out of control at home too, being an autopilot husband and an autopilot father taking everything and everyone for granted. My home had become a treadmill, a self-created one where every day was the same, nothing ever changed and nothing ever got better.

I was neglecting my health, overeating, drinking too much, not exercising enough and treating my family like they were colleagues at work. Sitting in that traffic jam that day, Botley made me realise that I needed to change – to be a better husband, a better father, to be a better person for myself and lead a more inspired, harmonious and fulfilled life.

He made me realise that I needed to have a sense of purpose and that to have everything I ever wanted, all I needed to do was wake up. The hamster was right, I needed to get off the wheel, I needed to set myself free to grow again and everything would be fine.

Five years later I was not only 'free' financially, emotionally and intellectually but even starting to become spiritually free.

This book isn't about quitting your job, but it is about quitting living your life unconsciously, on autopilot, tiptoeing your way safely to death. It's about not just hoping that everything will turn out ok. You see, hope is not a strategy; hope is great but it's not enough. Strategy is about awareness of who you are and what you are capable of. It's about understanding what you really want and more importantly, it's about the essence and ingredients of fulfilment. It's about stopping yourself from thinking about luck or just talking about success.

It's about living your best life to be healthy, wealthy, at peace and very happy. It's about being you, the real you. It's about harmony. These pages share with you my journey so far to harmony and fulfilment. As we all know every great journey starts with the first step. I invite you to take your first step with me. To achieve fulfilment and harmony you don't have to quit your job, but you do have to look at the whole of your life in a whole new way.

> *"People are like stained-glass windows. They sparkle and shine when the sun is out, but when the darkness sets in, their true beauty is revealed only if there is a light from within."*
>
> *Elizabeth Kubler Ross*

Chapter 2

Stop your wheel

"Many people die with their music still in them.
Why is this so? Too often it is because
they are always getting ready to live.
Before they know it, time runs out."

Oliver Wendell Holmes, Jr, US Supreme Court Judge

Yes, you read it right, stop your wheel. That's it; just stop your wheel for a moment. How hard can it really be? What I mean by stopping your wheel is just putting on the brakes and taking a little time out. Evaluate and take stock of your whole life, who you are, where you are now, across every area of your life, and more importantly, where you are heading. Are you on a collision course for mediocrity, regret and despondency or are you truly on the road to fulfilment in every area of your life? The only way to find out is to stop fretting frantically about the stuff you fret about every day and to metaphorically get off your wheel and take a good look around at what you are creating for yourself.

I know my wheel used to feel more like a runaway train and the thought of stopping it made me feel more than just a little uncomfortable. For some of us the very thought of such an outrageous idea can set in motion all sorts of neurochemicals we didn't even know we had. Ironically, in this situation most of our runaway trains are hurtling at incredible speeds on unfinished tracks, yet perversely it still seems easier and even safer not to stop. As Jack Nicholson once said, 'I'd rather stick needles in my eyes.'

After all, we have been on the wheel for so long, surely it must be less painful to stick needles in your eyes than to stop even for a moment. Anyway, why should you stop your wheel? This is the way life is supposed to be isn't it? Doesn't everyone live like this? Surely no one achieves any level of success without furiously expending inexhaustible amounts of effort. Aren't we all just human furless hamsters? So instead of stopping we stoke the furnace with a vengeance and accelerate even faster, eyes tightly shut, knuckles white and fingers crossed hoping for the best, oblivious and unconcerned about the end of the track because amazingly the pain of stopping to focus on where we are heading at that moment in time somehow seems greater than the pain of calamity further down the line. At this precise moment in time the future isn't real or at least it doesn't appear real. After all, we have so many other pressing matters to attend to. Future, buture, muture – who has time for future?

Who has time to stop anything? Getting through that project at work, meeting that deadline, paying for the new exhaust and how on earth are we going to manage the increase in mortgage rates? It's hard enough to just pay the bills and survive. Surely we have no choice but to keep running? It's all about catching trains, dodging the traffic and each other, putting ourselves first, worrying, complaining and getting away with as much as we can for as little as we can. As Yogi Berra once said, 'The future ain't what it used to be.'

For some of us it's about comfort eating, for some it's drinking excessively, for some it's devoting every waking hour to making the boss happy so that we can get home safely, buy a lottery ticket and watch TV with a glass of wine while we complain about how tired we are. For me it used to be all of the above. But hey, we get to do it all over again tomorrow and with a handful of exceptions you can guarantee that it's pretty much the same. All of this and we still say we are happy and believe it. If that's happy then I sure as hell wouldn't want to be sad. But how many of us are truly happy?

It's almost like watching a movie where the projectionist has a particular liking for one piece of the film, so takes it upon himself to continually rewind to that part. After all, it's his movie so he can watch what he wants! You wouldn't even put up with that once, let alone him doing it continually for the duration of the time the movie was scheduled to be run. Yet some of us will put up with exactly that concept for our whole lives, i.e. play the same movie over and over and over again. What's wrong with that? It's the way our parents lived and their folks before them. If the movie was good enough for them, then surely it's good enough for us we tell ourselves. The problem is, it's the same movie, and it doesn't take Einstein to work out that if you keep playing the same movie, at some point you are going to get really, really bored. You may even wear the movie out and find yourself stuck.

'We'll cross that bridge when we come to it'

Well, for some there's nothing wrong with being on the wheel, and that's fine; however, I happen to believe that there are many of us out there who want a whole lot more. My guess is that you fall into that category otherwise you wouldn't have acquired this book. If that's the case I'm delighted for you, because you deserve nothing less than the best life has to offer. Life is full of wonder and riches that are available to us all. No exceptions!

It makes sense to stop the wheel doesn't it, because isn't it just crystal clear that at some point in the not too distant future if your life is like that runaway train you are going to run out of track. Isn't it clear that it's going to end in pain, tears or at the very least bitter disappointment or regret? Well, it may be clear, but hell, it's a long way off so we don't have to worry about that right now, do we? Or at least that's what we tell ourselves repeatedly.

Anyway, it will probably be fine; things usually turn out ok. Another negative 'affirmation' many of us have got good at using. Like the old saying goes 'we'll cross that bridge when we come to it'. Have you ever stopped to think that to cross the bridge you need to build it first? It's your bridge whenever you need it, so you may as well start building it now so it's ready when you need to cross it. Incredibly, the thought of stopping your wheel seems as impossible as stopping your wife from buying another pair of shoes or getting your husband to put the toilet seat back down. Anyway, you haven't got time to stop anything, you've got bills to pay, lots of them, and it's the wheel that gets them paid.

At this point it's crucial that I emphasise that stopping the wheel does not mean you have to go out and quit your job tomorrow. What you have to quit is living on autopilot, sleep-walking through life, pretending you are happy. Stopping your wheel is about standing back, taking a huge long deep breath and an even deeper look at your whole life.

Don't wait for the shock or tragedy

In my experience there are only two things that can lead you to stop your wheel. The first is shock or some form of tragedy; the second is just making a decision to live life more consciously and taking action, massive action. Redundancy is shock! Having spent most of my working life in an office I have the very unpleasant memory of having seen countless numbers of people's lives turned upside down through re-dundancy. It's even something I had to endure myself at one stage and it's not pleasant. I have seen people let go who have held down the same position for over 20 years. For many of them it was their first and only job since leaving school so they knew nothing else.

For the most part it's never about one individual; it's often about an entire department or even the whole company. Each time I witnessed a redundancy programme I guess some-where deep inside of me, I knew it was the right decision for the company, although it never quite seemed like it at the time. I knew it was never personal, it was always strategic, designed to strengthen the organisation even though it never quite seemed so when the time came to let people go. Telling someone who had given 20 years of their life that they were no longer needed is one of the worst things you can either do to a person or have done to you. Setting aside all of the financial issues affecting the redundant person, one of the first basic human needs we all have is to belong and to be needed so to take this away from someone just stinks.

The reason for raising the issue of redundancy is that this is by far one of the most common causes of people stopping their wheels (or more appropriately having their wheel stopped for them). It creates shock – a massive 8.1 on the Richter scale shock. As difficult as it may appear, sometimes it can be a blessing in disguise, as I believe was definitely the case with a number of people I was unfortunate enough to witness being placed in that position.

One lady had worked for the organisation for 15 years; she was earning a good salary as a supervisor but was plagued with emotional difficulties. I know she received medication and counselling for depression and anxiety for two or three years prior to being told she was no longer needed. Life had already pulled the rug from half way under her feet and there she was just about to have the job finished for her by her employer. 'What would this do to the poor woman?' I asked myself over and over again. It was at times like this that I hated the organisation and had to question myself, everything and everyone around me.

The relevance of this true story is to tell you that what I had witnessed being done turned out to be one of the most precious gifts anyone could have given to another person (although I would never in a million years have anticipated that beforehand). You see, despite my anxiety and greatest fears, I learned many months later that the redundancy was a positive life-changing (and who knows possibly even a life-saving) event in her life. As a result of 'having her wheel stopped' for her, she was forced to wake up, stand back, take stock of her life and to get back on to the right track. What I learned was that not only had she got back on the track, she was living the life of her dreams.

She had taken the very small amount of redundancy money due to her, moved up to the North of England with her daughter to stay with an old friend and ended up buying and running a very small business which had been her childhood dream. I was also told that she was no longer under the doctor's care and was in every way imaginable a very happy lady.

Your wheel affects every single area of your life!

The point is that in the absence of that event, or something else to cause her to stop her wheel, that lady several years later, would still be spinning on and on and on in the same direction. The scenery may well have changed for her but it was more than likely to have got darker and more miserable than ever. So call it divine intervention or whatever you choose, the fact is, her wheel was stopped for her, resulting in a happy ending, but I know it doesn't always turn out that way. I know of many, many people still living unhappy or at best 'dull' lives because no one has stopped their wheel for them and they either don't know how to stop it themselves, or they are just too scared. The sad fact is that to have your wheel stopped for you normally requires a shock, or worse still a tragedy.

Please don't misunderstand me; I'm not just talking about work. I'm talking about every area of life and I mean every area. I mean your career, your relationships, your habits, your health, your personal and professional development, your growth, your stimulation, your social life, your spirituality, your environment, your bank account...Everything! Your wheel affects every single area of your life and it needs to be stopped occasionally so that you can take a bird's eye holistic view of the whole package. I have had my wheel stopped twice in my life and both occasions have had a profound effect on my life. Today it's something I regularly include on my daily 'to do list':

Monday – **STOP WHEEL**

Tuesday – **STOP WHEEL**

Wednesday – **STOP WHEEL**

Thursday – **STOP WHEEL**

Friday – **STOP WHEEL**

Saturday – **STOP WHEEL**

Sunday – **STOP WHEEL**

Having learned the hard way how important it is to stop your wheel, taking a very deep breath, standing back, taking stock and evaluating my life has now become a daily ritual for me, which I not only enjoy but it also pays enormous dividends.

Think back for one moment to a time when you lost something important to you personally, perhaps a piece of jewellery, your purse or wallet, keys, documents or something else of value to you. Do you remember the impact that loss had on you emotionally and physically? Do you recall the upset, frustration perhaps even anger with yourself? 'How could you have been so stupid?' you asked yourself. Didn't it play on your mind and haunt you for hours, days or even weeks? Didn't it bother you so much that you just couldn't help taking it out on the people around you who you loved the most? Didn't it dominate your every thought for a while, even if only a short while?

Now think about your 'average day', all 24 hours, each of the 1440 minutes, every one of those precious 86,400 seconds. Considering that each and every one of those moments has now gone forever and can never be returned to you, except perhaps in your memory, think about what you did with that day, what you did yesterday. Did you truly enjoy it? Did you relish every minute, every moment? What did you feel? Do you even remember how you felt? Were you happy, were you excited, were you thrilled, or were you confused, angry, frustrated or perhaps just on autopilot? Maybe you were just numb.

Whose lives did you touch and enhance? How did you treat the people you love most? How did you treat strangers? Did you make an effort to get to know anything about anyone? Did you smile at a stranger? How many times did you laugh? Did you laugh at all or attempt to make anyone else laugh? Were you guided or helped in any way by anyone, or did you guide or help anyone in any way? Did you complain, did you moan? How many of the things you set out to achieve did you actually achieve? Did you set out to accomplish anything? Did you feel alive, did you feel stimulated in any way, and did you do anything differently to the day before? Did you come up with a new idea? Did you tell yourself you couldn't do something? Did you read or see something you really liked?

How do you see things?

Did you look at other people as people, I mean real people rather than purely as colleagues, or bus drivers, or shop assistants, or just your wife or husband, son, daughter, mother or father? Did you set a goal? Did you think about your dreams? Did you feel your passion? What is your passion? Did you look at the sky, the ground, the trees, the birds, buildings, or even technology? How many times were you amazed by either nature or science? Did you once look at your own hand properly or the rain? Did you think about how grateful you were for all of the good things in your life? Did you even stop for a moment to acknowledge what was good in your life? How many times did you think about the past, or the future? How many problems did you come up against and how many did you create? Whilst you are at it, how many problems did you solve? Who did you curse? Did they really deserve it?

When you think about yesterday, do you have any real memory of anything tangible, significant or in any way special no matter how tiny it was, or did you just get through it? If you were caught up in a traffic jam or shopping queue did you puff and blow and work yourself up into a mini frenzy, or did you just take a deep breath and think about any of this stuff? Bob Proctor in his brilliant book entitled *You Were Born Rich* says that 'the average person spends most of his time tiptoeing through life hoping to make it safely to death'. Well, did you tiptoe? Do you remember anything? Anything? If you were lying on your deathbed and you were offered a choice of having that watch, ring, purse or wallet back that you lost and held as so valuable all those years back, or the chance to live another 24 hours, which would you choose? If you chose the time then what would you do with it? I'm certain you wouldn't be choosing the wallet.

'Life is short'

My point is there is a very old cliché which we all use all of the time, but we use it in vain, because I believe we are rarely truly conscious when we say 'life is short'. The very moment we've said it we then go on to waste it again...how does that work?

I experienced my first epiphany in 1994, when on 15th January I held my father's hand to watch him take his last breath and then just a few weeks later I held my newly born son in my arms. I went from total depression to absolute joy in just a few short weeks. It was then that I first woke up, realising that there was something much bigger going on around me and that I needed to 'wake up and smell the coffee'.

This thing we live in called the Universe is a phenomenal place and I didn't even begin to understand the world around me. I took practically everything for granted; it was time to change and I did. I was truly sleepwalking my way through life; I was exhaustively treading my wheel and the worst of it all was that I was barely conscious. However, whilst those events had an enormous impact on my life, it still wasn't enough. It wasn't until I saw myself, and so many other people that I cared about, living life like a hamster that the penny finally dropped. Then I really stepped off my wheel and woke up.

So the first step on the journey to harmony and fulfilment is to simply stop your wheel. I mean really stop the wheel. It doesn't matter what it takes, just do it. Find a way, your way, whatever it takes. Make the decision to lead a more conscious life; make it today and do it. The rewards are beyond belief and are there for everyone for the taking, but first you need to decide, then you need to take action and never stop taking action.

I know it's not just about work, because I know people who have treated their most precious relationships like a treadmill year after year, only to suddenly have their wheel stopped for them when their partner up and left them. It happened to a good friend of mine. After 30 years of marriage his wife left him; she was fed up with the treadmill and he didn't even see it coming. The divorce rocked his whole world and all because he never took the time or energy to stop his wheel every now and again and take stock of his relationships, especially his marriage. It's not because he is a bad person; in fact, he is a good man, and a good friend. It's just that in my view neither of them really took the time to stop their wheel. Now, I know of course, some will say that they could have stopped the wheel and it may well still have ended in divorce, but I guess that's something that we will never know now.

It's not just about relationships either; the wheel revolves around every single area of our life, especially our health. Most of us sleepwalk through life thinking we are invincible, immortal and that ill health and bad things only happen to other people. Well, the reality is that unless you stop your wheel from time to time and take a good long hard look at yourself you will find that ill health and bad things don't just happen to other people. I have lost count of the number of people I know who have had their wheel stopped for them through the shock or tragedy of ill health caused by the neglect of their very own bodies.

My own father drank and smoked himself to cancer, then shocked by the tragedy of realising he had done irreparable damage, he had his wheel stopped in the most irreconcilable of ways...death at the tender age of 66, when he should have been enjoying his retirement. He had even forfeited his right to see some of his grandchildren born. A good friendof mine drank himself into oblivion over a period of many years until he landed himself very seriously ill in hospital. The doctors stopped his wheel in an instant by telling him that his continued drinking would result in his imminent and painful death. Thankfully, he listened to the doctors, changed his ways and survived, but the sad reality was he had to have his wheel stopped for him when it was nearly too late. Luckily he made it.

The world is truly changing

Don't wait for the shock or tragedy; don't wait for someone or something to stop your wheel for you. The best gift you will ever give yourself, in your entire life, is to stop your wheel. This entire book is designed to help you wake up, but there is a caveat. There isn't a silver bullet, there's no magic wand, only desire and action which when applied in vast quantities together can truly give you everything you could possibly want from your life.

But remember, first you have to STOP YOUR WHEEL – don't wait for someone or something to do it for you. As the guys in the sports business say, JUST DO IT!

For the last 6000 years, all of the greatest thinkers, the greatest leaders, the greatest scientists, the greatest philosophers and every individual or organisation who has ever achieved any real level of success, have had to stop their wheels from time to time to take stock of where they were in relation to where they wanted to be. If you just keep doing the same thing over and over again expecting different results I'm here to tell you, in no uncertain terms, that you are crazy and you need to wake up.

You see, we live in a rapidly changing world where we have seen more change in the last 150 years alone than in the whole history of the world. Nothing, but nothing stays the same for long; everything is changing and we have to change too. We have to get off the treadmill if we want to thrive let alone survive. Technology and communications alone are changing at a pace almost beyond belief and it's just a fact that if an organisation is doing business today the same way it was doing business five years ago, it will very soon be out of business. If an organisation is marketing its business the same way it was five years ago it will soon be out of business. If an organisation is leading and motivating its employees the same way it was five years ago, it will soon be out of business. Everyone has to stop their wheel and take stock from time to time. What are organisations, if nothing more than a group of people organised to achieve a specific goal and any organisation which blindly stays on the treadmill, without stopping its wheel from time to time, is destined for failure.

Are you living your life the same way you were living five years ago? What will happen if you stay on your treadmill doing the same thing for the next five years, never changing? Maybe your wheel is the relationship that needs some attention or the overeating or drinking that's causing health problems. Maybe it's loneliness, boredom, frustration, confusion, doubt, sadness... Where will it take you in five years if you don't stop your wheel now and find a way to deal with it? The way to deal with it is through these pages.

The world is changing! So stop your wheel and change with it. This entire book is about stopping your wheel, how to do it and where to go from there, but the very first step is about decision. To stop your wheel you must decide to stop sleep-walking your way through life and to stop, stand back and take a long hard look at who you are and where you are, and to then truly wake up and live a more conscious life. I have some great news for you: having taken the time and trouble to acquire this book and read up to this point you have already begun the process of stopping your wheel.

"Slow down and enjoy life. It's not only the scenery you miss by going too fast you also miss the sense of where you are going and why."

Eddie Cantor, Comedian

Chapter 3

Wake up

"The best way to make your dreams
come true is to wake up."

Paul Valery

Ok, so now you've finally stopped your wheel, after all those years, all that energy, and all that effort. I guess it feels a little weird, maybe you even feel somewhat dizzy. Perhaps you feel uncomfortable, confused, lost, or even a little lonely because everyone else is still running furiously on theirs. Don't worry, it's perfectly normal!

First things first, you have stopped and you need to give yourself a huge amount of credit for that, because it takes real courage, real strength. The great news is that it's really the toughest part of the journey so you can know, that just by taking that very first step, you are already well on the way to success and living the life you not only deserve to live, but were destined to live. Having stopped you must at least be half awake, so now all you have to do is take a deep breath and open the other eye, because you need to become fully wide awake before we can move on.

Whatever your age, size or shape, I want you to look in the mirror; that's right, take a long hard look at yourself, every inch, every blemish, every hair. Stand butt naked in front of the bathroom mirror if you have to, but it's time to see who you really are, not what you have become, but who you really are. Most people find it's not so easy to do, taking a long hard look at every inch of yourself, looking into your own eyes, your own soul. Do you like what you see? Are you happy with your 'temple' or have you neglected it over the years? I know when I first did it I was very unhappy with what I saw. At first I didn't even recognise me, my whole body was so different from the person I felt like inside. I stuck with it though and kept looking, and that's what you need to do.

I really had to look beyond the receding grey hair, the beer belly, hairy nostrils and ears and the lines across my face that I hadn't even noticed before. Most of what I saw physically I didn't really like but I had to look beyond it all.

At this stage I'm more interested not in what you look like, but getting you to accept YOU as an incredibly wonderful, special, unique being who is being carried around in this thing we call our body. It's the YOU inside I want you to focus on because self worth isn't about the body you have created or the home you live in or how much money you have in your bank, it's about realising just how priceless you are, regardless of what you look like at this moment. It's tough to take a long cold hard look at yourself, at your creation, your result of years of living life on the 'treadmill'. Most people won't even entertain the thought, but I can tell you it's critically important that you do, it's a vital step in the process of waking up!

I know it's hard because it makes us feel so uncomfortable and for most of us we know we won't particularly like what we see if we look closely, so why should we put ourselves through that pain. Well, the point is there are two key objectives in doing this: the first is to get in touch with the real you and the second is to stand back and see the fruits of your labour, what you have actually built. It's really important to understand that what you look like isn't who you are. It's just a reflection of all of your thoughts, feelings, choices and decisions up to this point. What you see isn't the real you so you can change your image if you are fed up with the way you look. I know, I know, that's easier said than done. Of course it is. Whoever came up with such a ridiculous saying anyway? Everything is easier said than done!

If you haven't already done so please do it now – look into your own eyes in the mirror, look closely and look long and hard; don't be afraid, it's only you. How does it feel to look at you, the real you! Look deep into your eyes until you find yourself; it's not an easy thing to do but I promise you it's worth doing.

Life is a rollercoaster and you have to know how to ride it!

How many times in your life have you looked to see the real you? Not the weight, flesh and blemishes, but that person inside that's always there but never gets too much of a say. The real you hasn't really changed; it's just the stuff around you that you call your body that has changed. What do you see, I mean really see? What do you feel? What are you thinking? Perhaps you are wondering where on earth all of that time has gone. Can you remember what it was like when you were a small child growing up, becoming a teenager and then turning 20, 30, 40, 50, 60 or maybe you are even 80 and reading this? Did it all turn out how you expected? Was it all fun, laughter and happiness along the way? Was it easy? Any regrets? Anything you haven't done yet that you should have or wished you had? Anything you've done yet which you just shouldn't have? How many mistakes? How many big mistakes?

Do you remember when you were a child and you felt invincible and immortal? All of those dreams; all of those big ideas, hopes, plans and expectations. Ok, so here you are. So what happened, did it all turn out the way you expected it to? You're awake now so you can tell it like it really is. Anything missing? Anything?

Are you living your dream life? Are you living, or are you just getting by? Are you surviving or thriving? If you were to rate every important area of your life on a scale of 1 to 10 with 1 being abysmal and 10 being magical, where would you place yourself in each category?. Life is sometimes called a 'rollercoaster'. So, as our mind works most effectively with images, I like to think of it as the rollercoaster of reality and have created an image for how you can look at your life. There are many different areas and categories of life and it's important that you choose the areas that are significant to you, but to help you on your way, here is how I decided to look at my life.

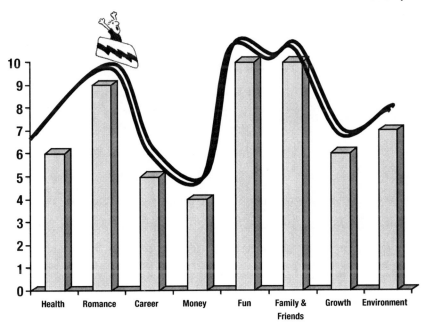

What's your reality? Is it more of a rollercoaster? Health, romance, career, money, fun, family and friends, growth, environment: these are the building blocks of life. Wouldn't it be great if they stood tall, erect and bold with strong foundations as they grew to reach for the sky? You see, the higher up you are, the more exhilarating it is, the cleaner the air and the greater the view and the advantage to see everything, all of the opportunities, all of the possibilities.

Are you a 10 in each of these areas? If not, what would it take to be truly a 10? If you're not a 10 but you have decent scores, are they at least in harmony? If these areas are not in harmony then what's missing, what do you need? Harmony isn't just important, it's absolutely critical. After all, what's the point of achieving financial freedom if you live a life that creates poor health, or you spend every waking hour earning to the point that you never get to see and enjoy your family. Money is a phenomenal tool and anyone who says otherwise is likely to have never had any or has misused or even abused its wonder, but it's only one part of the jigsaw of life.

I've met some people who have told me that they have no real desire to be a 10 in any or all of these areas and that they will settle for where they are and just accept their lot. Well, I guess that's fine, because I wouldn't want to force anyone to do anything they absolutely didn't want to do; however, my own view is different. I believe that it is our absolute right and our purpose to achieve a 10 in every one of these areas of life. I also believe that it's part of the fun, challenge and universal expectation of life that we play the game to get the highest scores we can. It doesn't mean we are self-centred or selfish, in fact to the contrary it recognises our own significance and potential to strive for excellence and be the best in all that we can do, be and have.

I think it's the most generous thing we could possibly do because imagine the joy, happiness, energy, excitement and enthusiasm we would project if we were a 10 or as close to a 10 as we could be in each of these areas of our lives. Just imagine the impact you would have on the world and everyone around you. If you need to, take your scores, look into your eyes in the mirror again, put your hand on your heart and ask the real you what's missing. Look at each rating you've given yourself for each category and whilst you ponder on that, look long and hard into the mirror of your soul. Ask the real you what's missing and what if anything is in your way. Take a few minutes to do this with each area of your life.

The point of stopping the wheel and waking up is to lead a more conscious life. To lead a more conscious life you need to be crystal clear on where you are today and where all of your thoughts, choices, feelings, decisions and actions have taken you. The good news is that it's not your past that creates your future unless like many people you live and dwell in the past. Most people are sleepwalking their way through their lives, there is just no question about it. They wake at the same time each morning, dress in the same way, eat the same breakfast, drive the same route to work to sit in the same job with the same people doing the same thing for the same salary, and come home from work and do the same things, in the same way, night after night in the same scenery with the same problems day, after day, after day. Nothing ever changes.

The hamster never gets a change of scenery…you can!

You are not a hamster! The hamster may have to live in a cage eating exactly the same food day in day out every day for the whole of his miserable existence. The hamster never ever has a change of scenery. The hamster may run endlessly on his wheel, always arriving back exactly where he started with nothing to show for the energy and effort expended, but that's not you. YOU ARE NOT A HAMSTER. The difference between you and the hamster, apart from the obvious physical distinctions, is CONSCIOUSNESS. You see, whilst a hamster will know he is in a cage, he doesn't really know that he knows he is in a cage. I'm sure a hamster must have thoughts, although I am pretty certain he is not conscious of his thoughts and his ability to think. You see, it's all about awareness and we have an unlimited potential and capacity to be aware of ourselves and the entire world around us, yet many of us still choose to live unconsciously.

What I mean by this is we wander around the planet doing the same things, thinking the same things and feeling the same way over and over and over again, just like the hamster running on the treadmill. We can change our lives in a heartbeat, in an absolute instant, but we don't.

So it's time to become conscious, it's time to wake up, I mean really wake up. One of my many favourite books is Jack Canfield and Mark Victor Hansen's *Chicken Soup for the Soul* which is full of brilliant inspirational short stories. One story by Price Pritchett talks about a man sitting in a hotel room observing a fly.

The fly is making desperate attempts to fly through the glass of the window pane without success. The story notes how impossible it is for the fly to get through the glass yet it never gives up and how through sheer effort it will die on the window sill. The point of the story, however, is that 10 small steps away a door is open to the outside world and the fly could easily be free. You see, the fly, like the hamster, does not boast the level of consciousness that we do, yet how many times do we act like the fly and the hamster? How many times do we just carry on doing what we have always done, like the fly, hoping and praying that one day our efforts will pay off, yet unlike the fly, all the time having the capacity to just turn in a different direction and fly out of the door?

To wake up, all you need to do is to start to become aware; become aware of what's going on around you and inside you. This is where detail is important. When you look around you, look at the detail and utilise all of your five senses of sight, sound, smell, taste and touch; don't just take everything for granted as you usually do. Start to look at the people, the room, the surroundings, the colours, the sounds, the behaviours, the expressions, everything. Look at the opportunities, look at the possibilities and note how infinite they are. Look at all the different shapes, sizes, colours, cultures, occupations, levels of wealth, action, energy, hope, enthusiasm, joy, peace, fun, and activity.

Look at you, what you are thinking, how you are feeling, how you are behaving. Look at your beliefs, what do you believe? Look at the results and life you have created for yourself and compare this to the results and life you once thought you had set out to create. Look at it all. Look at your home, your clothes, your skin, your body, your bank account, your breathing, your job, your friends, your relationships. Look at your health, your values, your goals and dreams. Look at it all. Look at your energy levels, your habits, your communication. Look at what you tell yourself over and over and over again.

EXERCISE

Take a long hard look at your very own rollercoaster of reality; just how balanced is your life? Where are you on a scale of 1 to 10 in every important area of your life? If you haven't already done so do it now:

Your Health

Your Romance

Your Career

Your Finances

Your Fun

Your Environment

Your Family and Friends

Your Growth and

Personal Development

Everything we need is already there inside of us!

Think about when you were a small child; do you remember that time when you felt like nothing was impossible, that time when you had such big dreams? Think about how relaxed, how confident, how curious you were. Do you remember that Christmas Eve feeling, the only night of the year when you volunteered to go up to bed early because the excitement was just killing you and you just couldn't wait to wake up on Christmas morning to see what Santa had brought you? Do you remember the intensity of that curiosity and excitement? Just when you thought the feeling couldn't possibly get any stronger, you leapt out of bed on Christmas morning and ran down the stairs with all of your heart and soul to see if Santa had been. Just when you thought that was as good as it got you then got to open the presents.

What about the time when you rode your first bicycle properly, you know that moment when your mother or father let go and you soared like an eagle in the wind? Do you remember that feeling of joy, freedom, success, confidence and glory? My god you had done it, now anything was possible. What about your first kiss, your first job, first promotion, passing your driving test, getting married, or seeing your children born? The list is both endless and priceless.

My point is that many of us have had hundreds upon hundreds of positive experiences in our lives. Experiences which brought us to life, made us feel full of life, energy, hope and excitement; experiences which raised our confidence and self esteem, and that made us feel so good. It all seemed so natural and wonderful; life just happened and we were awake to see it. Then somehow someday it just changes without warning or recognition, we forget about all of the great things, great achievements, great feelings and we start to sleepwalk through life complaining and worrying. We get on the treadmill and tread harder to pay the bills, feed the kids and keep a roof over our heads.

We end up so rigid with fear and worry that we lose our energy, we forget about who we really are and all that we are capable of, and so we lose touch with ourselves. It's like having a best friend who one day moves away and you miss him/her dearly but life goes on and so do you. The difference is that best friend is you and so much time has passed with you worrying and complaining that you have forgotten who you really are.

It's time to wake up, because that best friend is still inside of you, still curious and excited, full of hope, energy and dreams. Your body may have grown and you may have aged and look completely different, you may have brainwashed yourself to think you have to stay on the treadmill, but once you stop your wheel, wake up and think (I mean really think!) life can be as glorious again now as it was all of those Christmas Eves ago.

You may think I'm crazy suggesting you make a decision to lead a more harmonious life. You may think I'm outrageous suggesting you set a goal for 10 in each area. The point is, I tell you these things because you are worth it, you truly are!

Despite any negative thoughts or limited beliefs of the past, you exist on this planet as a wonderfully unique and special creature and you should be a 10 in every area of your life. Your 10 though, not my definition of 10, or your partners, or the media. Your 10, the 10 that brings you joy.

How to wake up!

Once I made the decision to stop my wheel here are some of the things I did to wake myself up. I would recommend the following action to help you wake up:

- Set your alarm for 5am each morning for the next three days. As soon as the alarm sounds get straight out of bed (no hitting snooze or feeling sorry for yourself). Get up, go downstairs in your dressing gown and open the back door. Spend just 5 minutes outside, looking up at the sky, taking deep breaths and just think outside of yourself for a few moments. Realise the vastness and greatness of the universe and everything in it, everything you can see around you and everything you can conceive. Just wonder for a few moments how everything came to be, including you. If 5am is too much then step out just before you go to bed. The point is to find a time when all is quiet and most people are asleep.

- When you go to bed each night spend 10 minutes before you fall asleep reflecting on your day. Think about all the things you set out to do but didn't quite get there and think about all the things you did and said but didn't plan to do or say. Think about how you treated yourself and everyone you came into contact with. Think about how you felt, really felt, throughout the whole day and how you feel now. Are you happy with the way the day went, if not, what would you do differently tomorrow and why? Don't beat yourself up over any of it, just play the movie and promise to do it better tomorrow.

- Set aside a couple of hours to take a trip to your local cemetery (I know, I know, you thought this book was supposed to make you feel better not worse...trust me). When you get there spend an hour quietly wandering around by yourself reading the gravestones. As you do that don't think about the death of all of those bodies around you, think about the death of all the dreams. Think about all the excuses, all the worry and complaining and wonder how much it's helping those souls now.

- Spend just a few minutes several times each day getting in touch with how you feel, I mean how you really feel, not just what you are thinking but what you are feeling inside.

- A lovely idea I learned some time ago (I think from Lester Levenson and Hale Dwoskin's 'Sedona Method') is to pick up a pen or pencil and hold it in your hand, squeeze it tight, really tight and as you do so feel the object, its shape, texture, and firmness. Then think of the pen or pencil as an emotion, one you may feel often, anger, fear, doubt, sadness, worry, etc, and realise that the pen or pencil is just like any one of those emotions you cling to so firmly. Realise that just like the pen or pencil you can let that negative emotion go. Just open your hand and let it fall. Open your heart and mind and let the emotion go; recognise how hard you have been clinging to it and all you have to do is just let it go.

- Keep a very simple diary for one whole week recording a simple and bullet point summary of everything, absolutely everything you did every half hour of every day for that entire week. The following week sit back and review it and ask yourself how awake you really were in doing some of those things and just as importantly, ask yourself how much time you wasted.

- Rate yourself now on a scale of 1 to 10 on your rollercoaster of reality in every important area of your life. Don't put if off, do it now and be brutally honest.

Waking up is simply living life more consciously, being aware of who you are, where you are in each moment, how you feel in each moment and what you want... what you really, really want.

You get to see things clearly when you are awake

Have you ever made a decision to buy a car and the very moment you made that decision you began to see exactly the same make and model everywhere, I mean everywhere? You almost couldn't believe it, how strange is that, suddenly everyone seemed to be driving the car you just bought...in the same colour. There's nothing strange or weird about that at all, those cars had always been there, it's just that you hadn't brought them into your awareness until they became of significance. The moment that happened you couldn't stop seeing them everywhere.

Up until that point why would you have noticed them, they were of no significance to you; they had no meaning in your life so why give them a second thought. That's what waking up is about; it's about waking up to the significance of life...your life. Realising and appreciating the significance of your life and what you want from it. Once you have made the decision to increase your awareness and to live more consciously you start to see opportunities everywhere.

Can you imagine for a moment the impact on an organisation in the market today not operating in a highly conscious state? Imagine an organisation existing and functioning without clarity of purpose, without a vision, without knowing why it's doing what it's doing and what the consequences are. Imagine an organisation oblivious to the thoughts, feelings and behaviour of its own staff and its customers. Imagine it not being aware of its financials, its strengths, weaknesses, opportunities and threats. If you can imagine such a failure you can also see a disaster and an organisation destined for closure.

You see, to be on top of its game, to be highly successful, every organisation has to be fully awake; it has to be truly alive and conscious every waking hour. It has to be alert and attentive to what it wants and how it is moving towards that goal in any given moment, whilst all the time also conscious of where it's heading once it has reached that goal. Whilst it starts with the executive, that consciousness must extend to every single member of the organisation to enable them to perform their role to the best of their ability. Failure to do so leaves the company vulnerable, exposed, weak and destined for failure.

In Napoleon Hill's brilliant book, *Think and Grow Rich* based on a study of 500 of the world's most successful and powerful entrepreneurs, Hill speaks at great length of the need for consciousness. 'Man, alone, has the power to transform his thoughts into physical reality; man, alone, can dream and make his dreams come true.'

The very essence of Napoleon Hill's book is that the one thing that each of the 500 people he studied had in common was their understanding that they had the absolute power to direct and transform their thoughts. The secret, however, to doing this was living consciously. They were not amongst the many 'tiptoeing through life hoping to make it safely to death'.

Are you tiptoeing or are you ready to wake up and live life more consciously?

"Believe that life is worth living, and your belief will help create that fact."

William James

Chapter 4

Ask yourself three questions

"I have found that if you love life, life will love you back."

Arthur Rubinstein

I remember once hearing another brilliant speaker and teacher Jim Rohn ask his audience (which included me) three very important questions which I believe everyone should ask of themselves. The challenge is to be brutally honest with yourself on all three questions (which I have altered slightly) and for some people that may be extremely difficult.

The first question you need to ask yourself is this: '*What will it take for you to fall in love with your life and be your own best friend?*' You see, I believe many people have yet to fall in love with their lives and don't fully realise the importance of doing so. I myself waited until the age of 31 to find this out. Prior to that age I charged through life on autopilot taking my life, my body, my mind, my health and just about everything and everyone around me for granted.

When I was in that hospital I held my father's hand whilst I watched him take his very last breath. I watched feeling totally helpless as he suffered and died before my very eyes, all the time realising we had never once told each other that we loved each other, or even how much we cared. I stared at him wondering how it was possible to love someone so much but not really know anything about them. It occurred to me that

I did not know my father. I had lived under the same roof as him for 21 years but I had no idea what he thought, how he felt, what he liked and didn't like. I didn't have a clue what made him tick, what his dreams and aspirations were, what made him scared or frightened. I didn't even know he was dying, no one did until he ended up in hospital. He had been suffering for months and didn't tell a soul he was dying from cancer, not even his own wife, my mother.

Just a few short weeks later on 31st March 1994 I held another hand in a hospital bed but this time it was my wife's as she gave birth to our beautiful son. I saw the most incredible sight I believe I will ever see – the creation of life before my very eyes.

The depth of love that I felt for my wife and son, for myself and for the entire universe in that moment was infinite. I knew in that very moment that my life would never be the same again; for the first time in my life I fell in love with my life. That gift was born through the love I felt for my father and the loss I felt as I let him go, and the love I felt for my son, as I welcomed him to the world and for my wife as she bore the pain of bringing him to us.

I knew all about birth and death before those two events in my life but I had never experienced either up close and personal. As I did for the first time I came to realise how little I really understood about life and the universe we live in. I began to wonder about who and what we were, where we came from and where we were going and why we were really here. I would look in the mirror or sometimes just look at my hand or even a fingernail and wonder as to the complexity of our creation. I knew then that I could never take myself or life for granted again. For the first time in my life I appreciated myself and everyone around me as unique and powerful creatures with infinite potential to create meaning in the world.

For the first time I realised it wasn't about what I looked like or how much money I had in the bank, or what job I did, or the car I drove. I realised I could have anything I wanted but it wasn't about that, I realised that **the meaning of my life was to give my life meaning**.

We are all incredible

I began to wonder what it took to create just one tiny hair on my head or create my eyeball or a tooth and then I'd learn about my brain and realise that my brain had some 10 billion, billion working parts, that it could store 100 trillion words and learn 10 new facts each second and that like most people I was wandering around the planet using at best 10 per cent of its capability.

I made a very important decision, a decision to learn about myself and what I was capable of and to grow. I knew that to achieve this, as difficult as it was going to be, my first challenge was to fall in love with my life, to stop complaining, moaning and sulking and to be thankful just for being here with whatever I had or didn't have in that moment. I learned a very important lesson, as Dr Wayne Dyer says, 'When you change the way you look at things, the things you look at change.'

It's amazing how your life changes when you fall in love with it, warts and all! I was overweight, unhappy, drank too much and stuck in a job I didn't particularly enjoy, but not for much longer. Things started to change when I fell in love with my life and become my own best friend. Here are just a few of the millions of reasons why I fell in love with my life:

Our heart beats around 100,000 times every day.

Our blood is on a 60,000-mile journey every single day.

Our eyes can distinguish up to one million colour surfaces and take in more information than the largest telescope known to man.

Our lungs inhale over two million litres of air every day, without even thinking. They are large enough to cover a tennis court.

Our hearing is so sensitive it can distinguish between hundreds of thousands of different sounds.

Our sense of touch is more refined than any device ever created.

Our brain is more complex than the most powerful computer and has over 100 billion nerve cells.

We give birth to 100 billion red blood cells every day.

When we touch something, we send a message to our brain at 124 mph.

We have over 600 muscles.

We exercise at least 30 muscles when we smile.

We make one litre of saliva a day.

In one square inch of our hand we have nine feet of blood vessels, 600 pain sensors, 9000 nerve endings, 36 heat sensors and 75 pressure sensors.

50,000 of the cells in your body will die and be replaced with new cells while you are listening to me.

There are 45 miles of nerves in the skin of a human being.

Our brain generates more electrical impulses in a single day than all of the world's telephones put together.

We are all standing or sitting on this thing we call earth which is 93 million miles away from the sun, spinning at 66,700 miles per hour around the sun and none of us ever fall off. So what will it take for you to fall in love with your life, just for the fact that you are here today reading this now? What will it take for you to be your own best friend, for you to love and cherish you just for being you?

The second question you must ask yourself is this: '*What are you like to live with?*' The reason this question is so important is that many people share a home with someone else or a number of other people and they become so wrapped up in themselves and self-centred, that they have little or no real regard for people living under the same roof. I believe that if you have made a decision either consciously or unconsciously to share a home with someone, you have an absolute obligation to both them and yourself to be a joy to live with.

If nothing else, let's be brutally honest, who on earth wants to live with someone who is always moaning or complaining, sulking or bitter, selfish or insensitive and unkind.

If you live under the same roof as someone you should commit to asking them to spend some quality time writing a comprehensive list of all of the things they love about you and all of the things they really dislike about you and could do without. Let's be clear this is not an easy thing to do as no one likes criticism, but believe me it's critical. If you don't ask, how can you ever expect to know, and if you don't know how on earth can you begin to fix it? I have seen marriages end after 30 years with the departing spouse saying they left because they were very unhappy for the last 15 years and couldn't put up with it any longer. No prizes for guessing what the missing ingredient is here… Communication! If you don't ask you will never know. You must be a joy to live with and if you are not, you need to find out why and fix it. Just imagine the magic of a relationship where those engaged in the relationship absolutely love each others company. Just imagine the joy, magic, success and phenomenal return you will get from a relationship where you are a joy to live with.

Like so many other things in life, this is one of those that is easier said than done. That may be true but it's worth doing. I should know because I would be the first to put my hands up to say my wife would not always say I am a joy to live with. What I can share with you is the fact that because I am so conscious about how important this is I am always trying. I know I often still get it wrong but I want my wife and son and family to be truly happy in my company so I always make an effort to be a joy to live with. I have made a decision to never stop trying no matter how many times I get it wrong. Every now and then I get it wrong and I make it my personal business to try harder.

The best way to do this is to really be there for those you share a home with; don't take them for granted, instead look for opportunities to be kind, caring and helpful. Some people pay more attention to the maintenance of their car or home than they do to the ones they love. It's all about energy; put as much energy as you possibly can into each of your relationships. Energy and enthusiasm are infectious qualities and if you exhibit these without drowning someone they will respond with energy and enthusiasm. Here are some simple tips for making this work:

- Never expect someone you live with to read your mind – you need to tell them! Also don't try to read their mind, ask them.

- Never expect someone you live with to be responsible for you or your happiness.

- Don't have impossible expectations.

- Go out of your way each day to do something helpful for them.

- Don't try to change someone you live with.

- Don't make assumptions about anyone and never judge them.

- Make them feel special and important.

The real point here is that if you fall in love with your life and consciously make an effort to be a joy to live with, so many other things just seem to fall into place. If you stop pushing, fighting, forcing, challenging and resisting all the time everything goes your way.

The third really important question is: '*What are you like to work with?*' When was the last time you asked someone to tell you what you are truly like as a colleague, boss or employee?

I know of no better way of doing this than participating or instigating an exercise of 360 degree feedback. The process works like this: you have a very carefully designed questionnaire highlighting many different areas and aspects of your behaviour, personality and performance at work and give it to as many people as you can to complete anonymously. You give a copy to your boss, copies to people who may report to you, copies to people who you regard as peers and anyone else who is willing to complete one that you believe could give you honest feedback. The absolute key here is complete honesty and anonymity.

When the questionnaires come back, that's when you get your answer. This exercise isn't for the faint-hearted; you absolutely must be able to take criticism and there will be criticism whether you like it or not.

Relationships are relationships whether at home or at work and given that most of us spend more time at work than we do at home, doesn't it make sense to create the most enjoyable working environment that you can. How much more fun and productive would it be if everyone made an effort to be a real joy to work with. Sadly many working relationships are quite superficial as office politics come into play. Many people expend so much time and energy fearful of losing their jobs or operating in a blame culture quick to point the finger at so called 'friends' when things go wrong.

Like any relationship it's all in the quality of communication. You see, life is a 24 hours a day, 365 days a year conversation. We are always talking to someone, if we are not talking to our family or friends it's colleagues, customers, shopkeepers or strangers. When we are not physically taking to someone else we find ourselves talking to ourselves and when we are not doing that consciously, unconsciously we are talking to ourselves in our sleep in the form of dreams.

So as life is one big conversation we owe it to ourselves to get good at it and if we want to get the best out of work we have to get good at being a joy to work with.

If you have staff working for you in any capacity then this is even more critical. It is a mortal sin to have people working for you and not to be a joy to work with. How can you possibly expect to motivate, lead and inspire people to be brilliant when you are not a joy to work with? Equally, what right have you to be in charge of people if you are always miserable, aggressive, moaning or complaining or even just keeping yourself to yourself?

Having spent most of my life working in the corporate world it always used to amaze me how so many managers and directors took their staff for granted forgetting their staff had lives outside work. I would see managers treat people like children yet the same employees might be parents or grandparents leading very responsible, creative and talented lives outside of work – although you would never guess this was the case from the way the boss spoke to them.

I'll never forget one of the very first seminars I attended many years ago where Tom Peters (author of *In search of Excellence*) was the presenter and he shared a story about how you can go into just about any company and talk to 20 people on the shop floor at the real sharp end of the organisation. He said that for the most part you will find that these people are extremely talented, creative and responsible individuals, yet many managers wonder how they get to be so talented and responsible, apart from the 8 hours a day they are at work.

Being a joy to work with pays enormous dividends in so many different ways. Not only does it invite more fun, laughter, balance, harmony, productivity and team spirit, it can help you climb the ladder to success in an organisation very, very quickly. Think about some of the most successful organisations on the planet. Think about them in relation to these three questions. Well, I don't know of any extremely successful organisation which would not go out of its way to declare its undying love for itself and create every opportunity to tell the world how it is the best organisation around.

How about the remaining two questions, you know the ones about being a joy to live and work with? Well, once again the best organisations in the world attribute much of their success to the way they regard and treat their employees. Now I accept that even the best organisations will still have a few disgruntled staff but the one thing you can be certain of is the highly successful ones care about what their staff think and they do go out of their way to ensure that it is a joy to work for that organisation.

All you need to do is to examine the culture of the brilliant organisations; look at their values, their vision, and how they treat people, both their staff and customers. Understand what they stand for and how they live their purpose and you will clearly see that they understand the importance of these questions on a personal level and strive to apply them on a corporate level.

"Dost thou love life? Then do not squander time, for that's the stuff life is made of."

Benjamin Franklin

Chapter 5

Decide your purpose

"As far as we can discern, the sole purpose of human existence is to kindle a light in the darkness of mere being."

Carl Jung

Unfortunately when we are born we don't come with a user manual; we are not like a DVD player or MP3 player, we don't come with a set of instructions and a 12 month guarantee. No one knows how we really work, not even our parents despite the fact that they think they do because their parents did before them and so on. We are extremely sophisticated, intelligent, complex creatures with infinite potential to achieve amazing things. I don't believe that we arrive on the planet and land in our mother's arms with all of the baggage we end up with 20, 30, 40 or 50 years later. We are not programmed to feel all of the fear, doubt, worry and anxiety that so many us inevitably end up feeling.

I believe we are programmed for love, joy, happiness, creativity and achievement, great achievement. The trouble is all of this other stuff we end up carrying around with us, we learn and the worst part of it is, that most of it is learned when we are just small children between the ages of 0 and 7.

So we have a massive challenge on our hands. In the first instance I believe that our purpose is to grow in every positive area of our lives and in and amongst the process of doing that, we also have to find a way to grow through all of the negativity that is dumped on our doorstep. We have to grow through the doubt, fear, worry and anxiety. The challenge is enormous, it's gigantic, but it's no greater than any of us are capable of. That's why it's how we choose to play the game that really matters.

One of the things I have noticed is that the majority of people never focus on purpose; they just drift through life focusing on results. They achieve one goal, and then move immediately onto the next without any real thought or consideration to what they are doing or going for or even why, it just feels like the right thing to do. That's all well and good, except for the fact that operating like this just keeps you on the wheel. If you have no clue as to where you are heading or why, how on earth do you expect to get there. Living in such blissful ignorance just makes you the same as my old hamster Botley; you just keep running and running with no end in sight – no purpose.

You see, it goes like this: most of us leave school having no real clue what it is we really want to do when we 'grow up'. We think we do and we may even tell ourselves we do, but with a handful of exceptions for the lucky few that do, we really don't. We end up in a job that our parents want us to do or choose it because it's the 'best we could get' or the 'pay's good' or 'the hours are good' or it 'seems easy enough'. There are lots of reasons for launching off in your first direction, but it's not common to find too many people who launched into a career because they were certain that choice would give them the challenge, stimulation, satisfaction, responsibility, continued growth and fulfilment that they not only needed but deserved. That's why staff canteens, water machines, trains, pubs, gyms and just about anywhere else you can think of are full of people complaining about their jobs. So many people hate their jobs, yet still go to work every single day terrified of losing their position.

Don't say you don't know…make it your business to find out

I remember a time whilst leading a team of staff at an insurance company when I sat down with one lady who had been in the very same job in that company for 10 years. The reason I did so was to congratulate her, express my admiration for her loyalty and find out exactly what she loved about the job that kept her so motivated to do exactly the same thing day in day out for 10 years.

Well, I remember being deeply disturbed for weeks by her answer, in fact I still think about it to this day. She told me that she not only hated her job but that she had hated it for the previous 9½ years and didn't enjoy any aspect of it. Now clearly very concerned and confused about her response I went on to ask her two further questions. The first was why if she hated it so much had she stayed for so long and was still there. The second was what, if anything, could I as the manager do to change things to make her happier. The response to both questions was 'I don't know'.

Worse than the 'I don't know' was the fact that I could see that she wasn't even prepared to put any effort into thinking about either of those questions. She was that runaway train; she was the proverbial hamster running furiously on her wheel. Sadly, though, she didn't have to run; she could stop and wake up at any time but she chose not to. She wasn't a bad person, in fact quite the opposite; she was an intelligent, sensitive, responsible and creative lady. She just had no idea of what she was capable of or what she wanted, so she let everyone else make her choices for her. This may sound extreme, but it's very true and worse still, I suspect that are many more like this lady out there 'tiptoeing through life hoping to make it safely to death'.

I remember in my first management job as a team leader working for an insurance company when they sent us on a leadership training course to develop the skills of becoming a highly effective leader. We spent three whole days on the course and there was no question that we learned a lot; however, on the afternoon of the last day the course tutor asked if we had any questions. At the time I was a little disappointed that he hadn't really spent any time talking about motivation. I wanted to learn how to motivate my team so I asked him, 'How do we motivate our staff?'

I wasn't really prepared for his answer which was this: '**The only people who need to be motivated are the people who can't see a future.**' That's right, '**the only people who need to be motivated are the people who can't see a future.**'

Well, I have to say I was even more disappointed with his answer. What a cop out, I thought at the time; how am I supposed to lead my team on that basis? Over the next few days I played his answer over and over again in my mind until I got it, the penny finally dropped. He was right, I thought, he was absolutely right. I suddenly realised that the only times in my life up to that point when I had really needed to be motivated was when I struggled to see where I was heading or how my efforts would pay off. I knew it came back to purpose.

I remember stumbling across a great piece of research that was done in the USA back in the late 90s. A team of psychologists and doctors set about a mission to study the secret of longevity. To achieve this they looked very closely at the lives and lifestyles of as many centenarians as they could find across North America and Canada. At the outset and during the course of the study the majority suspected the conclusions to be fairly obvious in that they would find that the secret was based on nutrition. They suspected it would be what these centenarians ate and drank throughout their lives and what supplements they took. They assumed it would be linked to them not consuming too much alcohol or smoking cigarettes.

The results, however, unearthed something they didn't quite suspect. Whilst nutritional factors and the absence of smoking and drinking too much were of course important they concluded that the two things that each and every one of these centenarians had in common was:

PURPOSE – each of them lived to such a ripe old age and continued to flourish because they had a sense of purpose – something they looked forward to, something they believed in, something that gave them joy and satisfaction. That may have been as simple as watching the sun rise and set every day or watching their grandchildren grow up or being there for their community. It was never about the size or scale of the purpose but about what it meant to them. They gave life meaning and purpose.

EXERCISE – each of them stayed as active as they possibly could. It didn't mean they went to the gym or went swimming, it just meant they kept moving.

When I talk to people about purpose many have a misconception of what purpose relates to. Some think it's a spiritual event where only the select few experience an epiphany at some point in their lives if they are really, really lucky. Some believe it's only something that Buddhist monks can tune into after years of mediating at the top of a mountain. Others believe that a purpose has to be a grand statement of ending poverty or world hunger or achieving world peace.

The Dalai Lama in his wonderful book *The Art of Happiness* begins the first chapter with the very first sentence as follows: 'I believe that the very purpose of our life is to seek happiness.' Well, if that's true, and I don't think any of us would disagree that it's a pretty good starting point, it's my personal view that the most effective route to attaining happiness is to establish:

- What gives you the greatest amount of joy, pleasure, stimulation and satisfaction than anything else on this planet?

- What would you do that would keep you up late at night and have you jumping out of bed early in the morning because you can't bear to stop and just can't wait to start?

- What would you do if you just knew it was humanly impossible to fail, if you knew there were no limitations in your ability or capacity to do it?

Whatever the answers to these questions are, you have found your purpose, and I'm willing to place a bet that you pretty much knew it anyway. If for some reason you still haven't got it and find yourself still struggling, try this. Think back, as far back as you have to if necessary, to those special activities or experiences in your life that gave you a heightened sense of being alive.

Think about those really special moments in your life when you felt brilliant, those times when you were making a real difference. The only thing standing between you and your purpose is a decision, but when you make the decision don't let it then overwhelm you by immediately reciting all of the reasons you can't do what you really want to do.

That's why most people never end up doing what they came here to do. Just relax and be grateful for where you have got to so far and know that your current results are not a reflection of your potential. We are going to explore how you get what you want.

The key is self worth and connection!

So let's look at this on a practical level – we want to drive an expensive car, to live in a big house and to own our own business. What's the point of any of those things? After all, they are all only things, and like us none of them last forever and we are clear that we can't take any of them with us, so what's the point? Well, the point is how we set about achieving them. The point is how we feel every moment of the journey, before, during and after. The point is how we think and how we feel. It's about how we manage our emotions and how we learn, grow and develop along the way. It's about how we create balance and harmony. It's about how we communicate and take others with us on the journey. It's about how we help others and how we serve others as we take every single step.

It's not about just the result; many of us have heard the tragic stories of some of the rich and famous who are desperately unhappy. We know of some of the celebrity alcoholics and drug addicts; we know of the suicides. They had it all yet at the end of the day when they were alone with themselves at night in bed it just wasn't enough.

You see, we need to talk about self worth and connection. It goes like this: results are the vehicle to growth. After all, to create a result you have to move, you have to take action, you have to think and feel and then actually do something. To grow you need to learn, develop and create, and if you go for positive results in a positive way, taking care to help and serve every step along the way, then you stand a pretty good chance of success. However, there are two critically important qualities you need to grow to achieve true joy and fulfilment. These are self worth and connection.

Self worth is about how you think and feel about you, it goes back to making a decision to fall in love with your life and stay in love with your life. It's about recognising that you are not what you have, what you do for a living or what other people think about you. Self worth is about how you perceive your place in this world and on this planet; it's about seeing beyond your size or shape, your age or colour, education or bank account. It's about losing the fear, doubt, worry and anxiety and recognising and appreciating the uniqueness of you and being thankful for just being here whatever your circumstances.

It's also about knowing that it is only ever you that creates your circumstances, and knowing that you can change any aspect of your life in a heartbeat because all you have to do is change the way you think and then you change the way you feel. The important point here is that self worth starts and finishes from within, not without. It truly is about how you think and feel; only you control that, no one else can. Now of course results can help, of course they can, that's why we are so preoccupied with them. Most of us only know how to raise our self worth by getting great results so we can prove to ourselves and the rest of the world how capable and worthy we are and that's fine, that's just great.

Remember though, that even with all of those things, you still have to think about how you feel about you, because they are just not guaranteed to bring you that joy and fulfilment. You may well have grown in the process of achieving the goal but in which direction exactly. Do you feel better about yourself, the same or worse?

Go for the results, really go for the results, go for growth and learn and develop and create, just do not make the mistake of kidding yourself that this is the route to a high self worth.

Never have just the end result in mind

This thinking starts before you get off the starting block. First you need to fall in love with your life and trust and believe in the uniqueness and value of you whatever your size, shape, colour, bank account or background. You have to love, trust and believe in you. Don't wait for someone or something to give you permission, feel it for yourself.

The other quality I mentioned is connection. What I mean by this is the opportunity connection creates for joy and fulfilment, to really connect with other people on every step of the journey so that you raise both your and their awareness. I don't mean just your normal day to day communication of being nice and polite, friendly and helpful. That goes without saying, but what I mean is really listening, empathising, trusting and going out of your way to make people feel special. That alone does wonders for your self worth. Doesn't that sound a little paradoxical – putting other people first and really trying to connect with them on a new level raises your self worth. Try it, it really works!

So go for results, go for big brilliant shiny results, and go for being the very best you can be, but don't get caught up in going for perfection, go for excellence. All the time you are going for the results think about your growth; think about how what you are going for will serve you in your growth on the journey towards it and once you have achieved it. Never just have the end result in mind and nothing else; otherwise there is just no point. Think about how it makes you grow, think about how it makes you feel, think about your self worth and how you can connect with others and raise their self worth.

When I first started to think about purpose a few years ago I became a little anxious. I had this belief that purpose had to be something hugely deep and meaningful and it wasn't something I could just decide, it had to come to me like an epiphany. I read hundreds of books on the subject and I began to believe that my purpose was preordained, written down somewhere in tablets of stone in the sky and I had to be truly enlightened and privileged to find it.

What are you drawn to?

I didn't want to meditate for years or shave my head so I decided to think about it differently. I began to believe that my purpose was what I decided it to be, but the underlying essence of whatever I chose was that it had to bring joy and give meaning to my life; it had to help me grow. When I talk about meaning it doesn't have to be something incredibly deep such as world peace, or feeding all the starving children in the world, it could be much simpler than that.

For me I knew I had a passion for personal development, communicating and leading and what gave me the greatest pleasure was getting results in my life and helping other people to get results too, so I have made that my purpose. While I was in the corporate world, all of those years sitting in management meetings, I believed my purpose then was to lead, so I guess I'm just looking to lead in a different way. It was always there, even though I didn't see it clearly; it was just something I seemed naturally drawn to in different ways. I have to point out though that I believe there is often a huge and also dangerous misconception that in order to live a life of purpose we have to leave our jobs and go feed the starving, build shelters for the homeless, move to Ethiopia or find a cure for cancer. These are all wonderfully brilliant, worthwhile and noble causes which many people are drawn to and make the decision to make it their purpose; however, many of us can find equally valuable and noble purpose in the jobs we find ourselves in. You may not be curing cancer or fixing poverty but you can find purpose in helping your children to learn, to grow, to smile, and to be happy.

You don't have to create world peace but you can inspire your family, friends, colleagues, your customers, your employees and even strangers. Many of us can find and live our purpose in any job. It's not the job we have but the energy and purpose we bring to it that matters. So maybe the purpose of life is to give life purpose – so don't wait for the epiphany, decide your own purpose today.

"I am here for a purpose and that purpose is to grow into a mountain, not to shrink to a grain of sand. Henceforth will I apply ALL my efforts to become the highest mountain of all and I will strain my potential until it cries for mercy."

Og Mandino

Chapter 6

Finish your story and move on

"He that is good for making excuses is seldom good for anything else."

Benjamin Franklin

Have you noticed how so many people have created their own personal story containing incredibly graphic detail about how they can't have exactly what it is they want? Many of these stories are best sellers and if taken on board by a Hollywood director and turned into a film, so many would be nominated for an Oscar. The stories are colourful, creative, imaginative and often so lifelike that sometimes it feels impossible to not accept them as the truth. Instead of the story beginning with that timeless sentence, 'Once upon a time' they start with a whole new introduction – 'I'll be happy when...'

The great Russian novelist Tolstoy captured this beautifully when he once wrote a short story in which some small children were told that the key to a wonderful life of happiness lay in their very own back garden. The children were told that the key was theirs to find and keep and that all they needed to do was to go into the back garden and search for it. The story, however, contained one caveat for the children: they must not under any circumstances think about a white rabbit. They were told explicitly that the key could be found but only if they did not think about a white rabbit.

Well, have you ever tried to think about not thinking about something! If you have and I know you have, you will know that it's absolutely impossible. To not think about a white rabbit you firstly have to think about a white rabbit. To then try thinking about putting it out of your mind the more you think about putting it out of your mind the more you end up thinking about it. It's impossible!

So the moral of this story is: when you say I'll be happy when I stop thinking about a white rabbit you will never be happy because you will always be thinking about a white rabbit. If you then apply this principle to everyday life you can see how it works. We decide that experiencing happiness, joy and fulfilment can only be achieved once we have achieved a specific goal first. The trouble is that to achieve the goal it is impossible not to firstly acknowledge the absence of the very thing you are looking to achieve. So, 'I'll be happy when I have lost all of this weight...' means there are two issues here, firstly, that you are not happy now and secondly, you keep thinking about your current weight and how it is holding you back from feeling happy. You have made a decision to postpone happiness.

'I'll be happy when I find that loving relationship I've been looking for...' means there are two issues, firstly, you are not happy now and secondly, you keep thinking about how lonely you feel now and how the absence of a loving relationship is holding you back from feeling happy. You have made a decision to postpone happiness. 'I'll be happy when I'm out of debt...' 'I'll be happy when I get that promotion...' 'I'll be happy when I get that car...' 'I'll be happy when I get out of this house and buy my dream home...' GET THE PICTURE!

You see, just like Tolstoy's white rabbit if you perpetually tell yourself 'I'll be happy when' you are programming your sub-conscious for not only postponing happiness and pushing it away but for accepting unhappiness.

It's all in the mind!

As a practising clinical hypnotherapist and having studied intensively the way our minds work, I can tell you that it works like this: we each have one mind but there are two vital parts of the same mind. Firstly, we have the conscious mind which is the part of our mind explicitly aware of everything that we are experiencing in the moment. The conscious mind has hard-wired into it our five senses of sight, sound, smell, taste and touch and in a nutshell that's largely how most of us experience the world we live in. We acquire information and experiences through the five senses and that's how we judge the world and the way we then live in it.

The conscious mind is the part of our mind that we use to think, to choose, to analyse, make decisions and rationalise. It's often compared to a captain of a ship whereby it's the con-scious mind which gives the orders and it's then down to the crew to carry the orders out. The manner in which the crew carry out these orders is often a direct reflection of their re-lationship with the captain. Well, in this metaphor the crew would be the subconscious mind. This is that part of our mind which contains information on everything that we have ever experienced since the moment of our birth; all of our memories and all of our feelings are stored in the subconscious mind. It's also very importantly the part of us that governs our habits and even our survival.

It governs our survival because it controls our heartbeat, blood flow, breathing, digestion and every other essential bodily function you can think of, including our entire nervous system. After all, you don't have to sit there all day long thinking about or worrying about how to breathe or make your blood flow or your digestion system work, your subconscious mind takes care of all of that.

Most of us live our lives through habit; we always eat the same foods at the same time in the same way, dress the same, speak the same, walk the same, drive the same, make similar choices and decisions in the same way that we always do, we even think the same things every day. Over 90 per cent of our waking consciousness and behaviour revolves around habit. All of these habits are stored in our subconscious mind and the subconscious is so powerful that often, even when we have made a decision to change some aspect of our lives through making a decision with our conscious mind, our subconscious doesn't readily respond to the memo. The reason for that is simply because we have told our subconscious the same story so many times, over and over and over again, that the subconscious treats the story in the same way it treats your breathing or heartbeat, it just goes on autopilot because that's what you have trained it do. It becomes habit.

So you see, when you repeatedly tell yourself 'I'll be happy when...' and then immediately carry on doing exactly what you've always done, you are doing two things. You are reaffirming to your subconscious mind that you are not happy and can't be, then you are imprinting on your mind a very strong image of lack and limitation. By saying 'I'll be happy when...' you are burning a picture in your subconscious mind of lack and limitation. It doesn't stop there though because what you are doing is choosing your thoughts with your conscious mind. Saying 'I'll be happy when...' is a conscious choice and decision which your conscious mind then turns over to your subconscious mind, which in turns generates the way you feel about that thought. Given that 'I'll be happy when...' is not a positive or constructive thought, it's inevitable that your subconscious, which is the 'feelings' part of your mind, gets a negative picture.

All your subconscious sees is the fact that you are not happy and more importantly, how far away you are from becoming happy, combined with the image of a ton of work to be done before you can even begin to get close to happiness. With such a dismal picture it seems hopeless and therefore you begin to feel helpless. The worst part of this idea is that this image then becomes a habit and as the negative image gets stronger and stronger it then only serves to influence your conscious thinking. You get so entrenched in this image that you then consciously and continually look at where you are in relation to where you want to be, you see the gap, you then see that image which you have created and accepted in your subconscious mind and you want to run for the hills screaming.

If it's not the 'I'll be happy when...' story then it's the 'I can't because...' story. It starts a bit like this: I can't because I'm too old, I can't because I'm too young, I can't because I don't have the money, I can't because I don't have the time...

The real problem with this story is as Henry Ford once said 'If you think you can do a thing or think you can't do a thing, you're right.'

You see, because of the power of your subconscious mind you become what you think about most of the time. Thoughts are things, thoughts are energy, so you really need to give some serious thought to what you are thinking about. If you are sitting there feeing sorry for yourself, feeling sad, feeling angry or feeling depressed, then just stop and ask yourself what you are actually thinking about. Guaranteed it will be negative, limiting, destructive thoughts. Guaranteed that if you change what you are thinking about and start thinking about something good, something positive, something you like or aspire to you will instantly change the way you feel. You may think it's impossible, but it really isn't, it just takes commitment and practice

A few years ago I flew to New Jersey to do the fire walk with Anthony Robbins. My wife thought I was going through a mid-life crisis wanting to walk over 15 feet of red-hot coals. For me, however, it was an extremely liberating, empowering and inspirational experience in my life. Up until that point if you had asked me to walk over a bed of red-hot coals I would have said 'I can't because it's impossible to do it without hurting myself'; however, I guess deep down I held that curiosity and wonder as to whether it could actually be done. Were the coals real? Were they really alight? Were they hot? Were they really that hot that they could burn? Were they fake coals? Were they coated in special chemicals that stopped you from burning? These were all questions that I asked myself. As soon as I got to training I quickly realised that everything was real, the coals were real and not only was there no special coating but that the coals were extremely hot. Many fire engines and paramedics were on stand by as testimony to the heat. Mr Robbins taught me that I would never complete the fire walk in a million years if I held in my mind the wrong story. Let me explain: what I learned during the training to enable me to successfully complete the fire walk revolved around three key areas:

1. **Physiology** – How I held, positioned and controlled my body had a direct effect on how I felt. In its simplest form, have you ever studied the difference in body language between a depressed person and one who is full of the joy of life? Their entire physical demeanour is hugely different; every single aspect of the way they hold their body and breathe is massively different. The depressed person looks down with shoulders and back hunched, has shallow breathing, looks limp and tired with nothing but a gloomy frown and sleepy eyes. The happy person, on the other hand, is bouncing around smiling, walking tall, shoulders back, looking strong happy and energised. The important point here is that whilst we know this to be true and also obvious it is a fact that if you change your physical state you can liter-

ally change the way you feel; if you change the way you feel you can change the way you act and do just about anything. Can you imagine what would have happened to me had I limped slowly, heavily, in a depressed state across those coals? Each day I walk firm, proud and tall, my spine erect and every part of me poised for purpose and greatness.

2. **Focus** – What I chose to focus upon in that moment would undoubtedly have determined my outcome. If I held a picture in my head of the coals on fire and the flames soaring high, with me stumbling and falling whilst I kept looking at the ambulances and fire engines in my peripheral vision, I might just as well have packed up and gone home. There was absolutely no way in a million years I would have even started the fire walk let alone completed it. I knew I had to focus on the outcome. I had to visualise myself getting to the end of the 15 ft walk triumphant and ecstatic, feeling great. I had to see myself walking along a lovely bed of soft cool moss. Focus was everything. I couldn't focus on all of the bad things that had happened to me in my life, all of things that had gone wrong, the mistakes, and the failures. No way! I had a choice as I do every second of every day and whilst doing the fire walk I chose to focus on success. Now each and every day I choose to focus on success and happiness.

3. **Language** – If you start the 15 ft walk across a bed of red-hot coals reaching over 1000 degrees Fahrenheit

telling yourself how useless you are and how you can never get anything right, you better make sure you've got plenty of health insurance because you are truly going to need it. You just cannot use language which denotes failure or negativity of any form. You have to say to yourself you can do it, everything is great, you are great and you know exactly what you are doing as you walk your way across that bed of cool moss to success. Language is everything!

So just stop for a moment to think about these three vital ingredients of success: physiology, focus and language. How do you rate yourself in each of these areas? What conversation are you having with yourself over and over again? How do you carry yourself during the good times and the bad? What do you spend most of your time focusing on? Start to pay attention to yourself; how do you carry your body around, how do you move? Notice what you are focusing on and how you are talking to yourself. Pay attention to all the negatives; it takes time and effort but I promise you it's worth every ounce of energy.

It all comes back to the story we tell ourselves

That's what I mean by your story. You see, it's fine to have a story, we all like a good story and in fact when we were small children we loved them, we couldn't get enough of them. Most of us prefer creative, constructive and positive stories with a happy ending; they were the essence of our childhood. Once upon a time anything seemed possible, we had such infinite belief and imagination, but somehow, someday it all changes and we start a new story, 'I'll be happy when', 'I can't because', 'if only', or 'someday I'll'.

The fact is all of these old stories are fiction, they are just not fact. Each of them has been created by false beliefs and because you have read your own story thousands of times you have begun to believe it, but it's just not true. It's a universally accepted fact that if you tell yourself the same lie over and over again one day you will not only find yourself believing it, but you will find yourself acting it out. Look around the world at the millions of successful people that walk amongst us and strip everything back to basics; look at who these people are, look closely, real close. They are all essentially the same as you and I, everyone born with the same infinite potential, the only difference is how we choose to maximise or ignore that potential.

It all comes back to the story we tell ourselves. Ask anyone at the very top of their field or profession what they tell themselves everyday and you will hear a great story, not a destructive, negative disempowering one. Ask them to truthfully tell you whether at any point on the journey they have doubt, fear, worry or anxiety and unless they are lying they will tell you of course they do. The difference between them and other people who are at the other end of the success spectrum is the story they tell themselves when they experience these inevitable human challenges. You may have grown up in an environment where you heard the same negative stories over and over again: 'I'll be happy when', 'I can't because', 'if only', or 'someday I'll'. You may even have been told repeatedly that you were no good or would never amount to anything. But guess what, these are not your stories; they belong to other people and now it's time to create your own new empowering, positive story. Make sure it's one with a happy ending.

So please make a commitment to finish the old negative destructive story and start a new healthy, positive, constructive, empowering story. While you are thinking about your story here are a couple of things you really should watch out for:

YES BUT – These are two of the most destructive words on the face of this planet; they stifle creativity, innovation, success and imagination, in fact they only serve as a magnet for mediocrity and failure. Nothing brilliant was ever created by using the words yes but. How many times have you come up with an idea, a thought or a suggestion either to yourself, friends, family or colleagues and had it 'yes butted'.

Yes but, it will never work...

Yes but, we've tried that before...

Yes but, what about...

Yes but, that's not the way we do things...

Yes but, that's not me...

Yes but, I can't because...

Yes but, yes but, yes but.

A number of years ago I was leading a very successful operation in the North of England, an operational team of about 300 people working across a whole range of disciplines.

There were six other similar operations spread geographically across the whole of the UK and we had some of the best results across all of the performance indicators in the whole country. One day I received a call from the vice president of the company asking me if I would like to move to London to run an operation twice the size but with the worst results in the country. He had explained to me that they had tried everything possible to turn the results of the operation around without success and that if I could not 'fix' it they would have no alternative but to close it down.

I accepted the challenge and a few short weeks later packed my bags and moved some 300 miles 'down south'. I have to tell you these problems were far worse than the vice president had explained, as not only were the results across the entire operation awful, morale had hit rock bottom. These people were operating in a trough of despair and it was deteriorating by the second. It was so bad that I spent the first three months repeating a huge mistake, and I wasted so much time I could have shot myself once I realised what it was I was doing wrong. The big mistake was this: I wandered around the business asking everyone I could 'WHY?'

'Why do we have the poorest sales performance in the country...?'

'Why do we have the highest cost base in the country...?'

'Why do we have the lowest customer loyalty in the country...?'

'Why do we have the lowest staff morale in the country...?'

'WHY, WHY, WHY, WHY, WHY...?'

What an incredibly stupid question, although I didn't realise it at the time, I thought it was the obvious question to ask. Well, it wasn't and the reason for this was that I learned that every time you ask someone why they give you a reason, their reason, their story. You then have to go through the pain of trying to firstly work out whether the reason is valid and if it is, you then have to work out what you are going to do about it anyway. So after three months of very painful 'WHYING' people, I decided to stop because I had given myself a desk full of literally hundreds of reasons why the operation was failing and all I had achieved was to get people even more focused on the problems than they already were. So I had to find a new question and it was this: 'WHAT are we going to do to turn this around?'

You see, all I had done for three months was to encourage people to share with me their own stories, when what I needed to do was to get them to think creatively and think of solutions. In the process of asking the new WHAT question I realised that the team was so programmed with the WHY that when anyone came up with any idea they immediately thought of a reason WHY it wouldn't work. They continued the old story that they were so used to. Whatever the idea, whatever the suggestion no matter how brilliant or obvious, you could guarantee that someone somewhere would kill it dead in a heartbeat with those fatal words...YES BUT! I knew it was time for this to stop, we had already made a quantum leap in not asking why, but now the WHAT was being stopped dead in its tracks.

I commissioned a toy maker to create for me hundreds of soft stretch balls with the words YES AND... written all over them in very big, very bold black letters. I invited every one of the 600 members of staff to a local theatre and in the process of presenting a number of strategic ideas to turn the whole business around based on their own suggestions from the WHAT question, I gave each and every one of them their very own stress ball with those words YES AND printed on them. I explained the problem whereby the team would never make any progress in improving their results and regaining the pride they once all felt in their region, if they maintained the debilitating culture of YES BUT.

They were all instructed to carry their YES AND ball with them at all times whilst they were working. They were told that if ever they or any of their colleagues came up with an idea or suggestion no matter how small or how stupid it may seem at the time, if ever anyone 'YES BUTTED' the idea, they were all to throw the stretch ball at the offender as hard as they possibly could.

Initially they thought that both I and my idea were nothing less than insane and that it was childish and would never work. After a little persuasion, however, they agreed to give it a try. Well, the rest is history, after the next three months of these balls flying everywhere, we soon replaced the words YES BUT with 'YES AND it's just possible that that may work, let's explore it'. One year later the region had moved from bottom place in every key result area to within the top three and sometimes at the top.

ENERGY THIEVES – When I was a young boy I used to love to stay up late at night to watch the old Dracula movies. Of course I knew there was no such thing as vampires that sucked your blood and drained you of every ounce of your life force but like most fiction when you are a young child I guess you can just never be that 100 per cent certain.

Well, I guess I was right to retain that miniscule level of doubt, because as I grew up and turned into an adult I soon began to realise that there was a form of vampire that walked this earth. They weren't the type from the old films though, the ones that sank their long spiky teeth into you and sucked your blood, no, these were far more sophisticated. These creatures looked just like you and I as the vampires did, although they didn't have really pale faces or pointed teeth, they looked quite normal. There was one major difference: they didn't drink your blood but they still managed to drain every ounce of energy from you by just talking to you. That's exactly what energy thieves do; they are highly skilled at talking you to the point of exhaustion and depression. The worst of it is we all know some of these people; you may have one at home or at work or a close friend – it may even be your mother! An energy thief is someone you know who will go to great lengths to tell you their own story as often as possible and spend every ounce of their energy complaining, moaning, whinging, feeling sorry for themselves or competing with you to explain how their day was much worse than yours.

Energy thieves love to wallow in self pity, the problems, failures and despair of life but they are only ever at peace when they are sharing all of this negativity with someone. They love a good negative story. They will spare no effort in going into as much detail as humanly possible and you can be certain that despite the façade they are not interested in help or advice; they will quickly ignore it as they move on to tell you the next problem. The irony is that by the time you have spent 10 minutes either in person or on the phone to an energy thief they leave you to go off themselves feeling in a brilliant mood, full of zest, energy and with enough excitement and enthusiasm to move on to their next victim. You, however, are left drained, exhausted and lifeless…

It may just have well been a vampire sucking your blood, because by the time they have finished with you there is nothing left of you. Be aware you can meet these people anywhere, I mean anywhere, and you can't spot them until they open their mouth and you find it's too late. Now the significance of this point is to explain to you that these people are simply storytellers and they always have and will always love to share their story, but it will always be negative, Your role is two fold, firstly, to avoid them like the plague and secondly, never ever to become one.

If you are unfortunate enough to have an energy thief in your life that you just cannot avoid then do yourself a favour: do not go to see or speak to them often and when you do make sure you do not stay or listen too long. I have managed to remove most of the energy thieves from my life now. However, as and when I come across a new one I make a point of telling them in the nicest possible way how they sound and what they are doing to themselves and others in the process. I do my utmost to work with them to help them change if I have to.

"All successful people men and women are big dreamers. They imagine what their future could be, ideal in every respect, and then they work every day toward their distant vision, that goal or purpose."

Brian Tracy

Chapter 7

Choose and decide wisely

"The strongest principle of growth lies in human choice."

George Eliot

'Choice consists of the mental process of thinking involved with the process of judging the merits of multiple options and selecting one of them for action. Some simple examples include deciding whether to get up in the morning or go back to sleep, or selecting a given route for a journey. More complex examples (often decisions that affect what a person thinks or their core beliefs) include choosing a lifestyle, religious affiliation, or political position. Most people regard having choices as a good thing, though a severely limited or artificially restricted choice can lead to discomfort with choosing and possibly, an unsatisfactory outcome. In contrast, unlimited choice may lead to confusion, regret of the alternatives not taken, and indifference in an unstructured existence; and the illusion that choosing an object or a course leads necessarily to control of that object or course can cause psychological problems.' (www.en.wikipedia.org/wiki/Choice)

'Decision making is the cognitive process leading to the selection of a course of action among variations. Every decision making process produces a final choice. It can be an action or an opinion. It begins when we need to do something but know not what. Therefore, decision making is a reasoning process which can be rational or irrational, can be based on explicit assumptions or tacit assumptions. Common examples include shopping, deciding what to eat, when to sleep, and deciding whom or what to vote for in an election or referendum. Decision making is said to be a psychological construct. This means that although we can never "see" a decision, we can infer from observable behaviour that a decision has been made. Therefore, we conclude that a psychological event that we call "decision making" has occurred. It is a construction that imputes commitment to action. That is, based on observable actions, we assume that people have made a commitment to affect the action.' (www.wikipedia.org)

Our ability to think and to use the power of thought to create choices and make decisions is by far the most precious gift bestowed on the human race. You only have to look around you to realise and appreciate that absolutely everything which wasn't created by nature started with a thought. The book you are reading now, the paper it is written on, the ink used, the chair you may be sitting on in the building you are in, the clothes you are wearing, the car you drive, the music you listen to, the TV and programmes you watch, the phones you use, the light and heating you enjoy, the carpet you walk on, bed you sleep in, toilet you sit on, aeroplane you fly in, train you travel in, knife and fork you use, etc, etc. You see, everywhere and I mean everywhere you look, everything you see started as nothing more than a thought. Our entire planet is filled to the brim and overflowing with products and services with thousands upon thousands of new ideas being created every single day all through the power of thought, nothing more and nothing less.

The exciting thing about this fact is that these thoughts are not exclusive to a handful of 'special' people, the rich or famous, the powerful or creative. No, not on your life, every single one of us has the facility and power of thought at our disposal every single second of every single day. The reality though and real question is, how many of us are conscious of those thoughts? How many of us know, understand and appreciate what we are thinking about at any moment of the day? Dependent upon which piece of research you read and choose to accept, you will find that the average person has anywhere between 50,000 and 70,000 thoughts each and every day. Now how it can be humanly possible to count these thoughts is another story, but I guess if we can send a man 250,000 miles to the moon in just a few short days and time the landing with the precision of a fraction of a second, then who am I to question how we can establish the number of thoughts we have in a day.

60,000 thoughts a day!

The point is we have the capacity to think, and through our thoughts we can not only radically change our own lives we can also change the lives of those around us and even the whole world. Look at what Edison did in thinking about creating light for us and how the Wright Brothers changed our world thinking about the kingdom of flight. Hey, but lets get with the times, what about Bill Gates! Of course the problem is that if we were to stop to monitor and analyse each of those 60,000 thoughts which run through our minds each day we would quickly become quite insane. I believe this is largely the reason why so many of us are not living lives as consciously as we need to in order to achieve a life of success across all areas of our health, wealth and happiness. We just have too many thoughts, don't we? That may well be true but how does that explain that amongst the six billion people walking the earth today, countless people have found a way to filter those 60,000 thoughts to lead successful happy lives. These people understand the principle of choice and decision, they understand that they may well have 60,000 thoughts flying through their mind each day, but they also understand that they have a choice of which of them to think about. They choose which ones to entertain and dwell upon. Equally they understand and accept their ability to act on those choices by making decisions.

I find it fascinating and extremely empowering to realise, accept and appreciate the fact that we can choose to dwell and focus upon any one of those 60,000 thoughts and we can even decide to create and choose new ones. What's even more exciting and liberating is that fact that whatever we choose to focus on expands so rapidly and so fully, that it seems to take only moments to dominate our lives. It's incredibly exciting, you see, the moment you choose to focus all of your energy and thoughts on your purpose one of two things can happen: either you think about all of the obstacles, the problems, issues, roadblocks, reasons and circumstances why you can't have what you want, or you think about all of the possibilities and opportunities. That's the power of choice that many of us either neglect or even worse, grossly abuse.

Out of the 60,000 daily thoughts some of them are really visionary, exciting and powerful whilst some are stifling, exhausting and destructive. So the question is which of the two types of thoughts do we choose to hold in our minds. Sadly, much of it comes down to habit. You see, as I have already noted some 90 per cent of our lives are led through us being on autopilot and that includes the choices we make. If we have historically spent most of our lives choosing to see the glass as half empty instead of half full, then it's highly likely that we continue with that pattern of choice for most of our lives, unless and until someone breaks the pattern, breaks the cycle.

What is it you choose to think about each moment of each day? Do you think about how unique, powerful and creative you really are and how you can do, be or have whatever it is that you may want? Or do you choose think about how tough life is and how the great things in life never happen to people like you? If it's the latter, then you need to make another choice and choose to understand where these thoughts come from and why on earth you, as a uniquely powerful and complex creation, would even dare to choose such limitation. If you choose to think like this you will see that just like smoking, excessive drinking or overeating, it very quickly becomes a habit. If you are struggling today in a big way it may well be that somewhere down the line some time ago you got the impression from someone or something that you were not good enough and you bought it. Unknown to your conscious mind you subconsciously chose to accept stuff you heard or saw when you were just a small child that suggested to you that you could never be good enough and you subconsciously began to act it out. Remember, repetition is the mother of skill and the more you told yourself that 'stuff' the more you began to believe it, right up to the point where you didn't even need to consciously think about it any longer. That thought pattern became a habit; a habit deeply embedded in your subconscious mind. If you do the same thing over and over and over again you create a habit. If you think the same thing over and over and over again you create a habit. Habits can of course be broken but only through using the power of choice and decision.

SMOKING KILLS! So why do people still smoke?

Have you ever wondered why smokers smoke? Every smoker knows that every single cigarette they light up and put in their mouth is filled with chemicals and poisons, which deep down they know are seriously harmful to their health. Despite this knowledge and the fact that the packets have written on them in big black bold capital letters SMOKING KILLS they continue to take a long slow deep drag of the poisonous fumes. These are intelligent, responsible people, so why do they choose to kill themselves slowly in this way? How does that work? Well, as a former smoker I can tell you that it works like this: most people start smoking when they are very young, in my case I was 15 years old and it was due solely to peer pressure. All of my school friends had smoked for some time but I had resisted it, due largely to the fact that both of my parents smoked at home and I hated the smell on my clothes. Despite this my friends put me under enormous pressure to smoke; I got teased and called names and generally made to feel quite inferior and definitely the odd one out. The smokers even got all of the girls, can you believe that! After a few months I cracked, I gave in to the torment and made a choice and a decision. I chose to become a smoker and decided to learn to smoke. To my surprise it was much harder than I had imagined. I managed to get hold of a packet of senior service cigarettes and took them to my local park, lighter in hand.

I lit my first cigarette, inhaled and coughed my lungs and guts up. Despite the fact that it was incredibly disgusting I had already made the choice and decision, so I knew there was no turning back. Once you have truly made the choice and decision the rest is easy, and it's then only a question of time before you make it happen. So I lit another cigarette and went through the same pain, then another and another and another, each as disgusting, as nauseating and as painful as the first, but I made my decision. I continued until the moment came when I got used to it, when it finally didn't seem quite so bad. Eventually it got to the point where it felt almost normal and I saw myself as a smoker. You see, what I hadn't realised at the time was that the human body isn't naturally built or programmed to poison itself with such toxicity and so each time I inhaled my body simply and naturally rejected the very process. However, because I had made a very conscious and determined decision to become a smoker, through the process of repetition I trained my subconscious mind to accept the new behaviour. My subconscious's natural instinct was to reject the smoke and the entire process, but my repeated lighting and inhaling of the cigarette was a means of my overriding the subconscious to instruct it to smoke.

Once my subconscious had accepted the instruction, that was it, job done; I had created a new habit. I had told my subconscious that not only was smoking perfectly acceptable, but that it was something I really wanted to do. As I have said before, repetition is the mother of skill and by forcing myself repeatedly to smoke I was developing the skill of smoking, even though it was poisonous and destructive to my health. I created the habit of smoking to the point that when I many years later made a conscious decision not to smoke, I couldn't give up. I tried everything but just couldn't give up. Once the command to smoke was embedded in my subconscious mind that was it, the only way to change the instruction was to penetrate the subconscious mind and reprogramme it.

I used all the willpower I could muster at the time but nothing seemed to work. It got so bad I remember a time when I lit a cigarette whilst wearing one of those stop-smoking patches on my arm – how crazy is that! I even remember the moment of my father's death, when I made a conscious decision never to smoke again because I had held his hand and watched him die of throat cancer because of smoking. Within an hour of his death I was outside the hospital grounds smoking, can you believe that! I had made the conscious decision as I had done many, many times before and even though I had witnessed my father's death, my conscious control was just not strong enough – I continued to smoke.

It was only a year later after the birth of my son when I found myself smoking out on the patio in the freezing cold rain, looking through the patio door at my wife holding my son, that I realised it really was time for change. This time, whilst it was a conscious choice and decision I drove it through to my subconscious mind through the power of my imagination. As I stood outside in the cold, wet, rain, I saw my wife playing with my young son and suddenly realised that one day when my son grew up he could be holding my hand as he watched me die, with me never having the opportunity to see my grandchild, his son or daughter. I created the image in my mind of my son holding my hand, crying, begging me not to leave him.

It's the image that drives change

The image was so powerful, it was devastating and compelling... so much so I knew in that very moment I could never smoke again. I knew that I needed to see my son's children. I knew I wanted to be a grandfather and to live a long healthy life playing with my grandchildren. I made a choice to hold that image in my mind always and I made a decision to stop smoking. Fourteen years on I have not only not touched a single cigarette but I must have reprogrammed my subconscious too well, because I now hate the smell of any tobacco; I can't even stand in the same room as a smoker. Now it's important for me to emphasise at this point, that I am aware that not everyone starts smoking in the same way and for the same reasons as I did. I am willing to bet though that a vast number of people started in a very similar way, regardless of their age. I'm simply trying to illustrate the following points:

- We have a choice in everything we say, feel and do!

- It's our decisions that shape the quality of our lives.

- Once you've made the decision the rest is easy. The person you need to speak with to make the choice and decision is available for consultation 24 hours a day; all you need to do is look in the mirror.

- If you keep telling yourself the same thing, keep doing the same thing, keep feeling the same thing, you are creating a habit through your subconscious mind.

- Trying to stop a habit just with your conscious mind is hard, you need to visualise and feel what you want.

- You must get the message through to your subconscious.

Why do you do the things you do?

Think about the choices and decisions you have made over the years. Why did you make them? Did you make them because you were scared and you wanted to avoid pain of some form, either physical or financial or emotional? Or did you make them to take yourself one step closer to pleasure or comfort? Whenever I find myself in a situation where I want to do something but find myself not doing it and don't really under-stand why, I take myself to sit quietly and think about it. I ask myself what pain I am trying to avoid and once I understand what it is that scares me I think about what pleasure there is to be gained by actually doing it and seeing it through.

It's not enough for me to just go through the conscious proc-ess, though, of working out what I'm scared of and what the benefits are; I need to focus on the pleasure, the benefits, and the positive outcome. The best way I know to do this is to use my conscious mind to create as strong and as clear an image as I can in my mind of all the positive things and all the good that can come out of doing what I've been avoiding. Once I have the image I have to hold it and make it as clear, bright and as colourful as I possibly can. I then generate the feelings associated with the good attached to it and I turn the image over to my subconscious mind. I don't just do this once though, I do it several times a day for several days or weeks, until it begins to feel natural for me to think in this new way of this new image.

I believe that everyone has the ability to visualise and if you doubt your own ability, just close your eyes and think about what your car looks like or your front door or living room, picture anything you are already familiar with and see what comes to mind. Whether it's a new job, relationship, car, health, money whatever you want, visualise it. See your-self at the new desk, or with the new partner, or spending the cash because you know it's there, see yourself slimmer, healthier, fitter.

What choices and decisions did you make 10 years ago? How have those choices and decisions changed or impacted the course of your life? What was so different then that through the power of YOU, you changed? What choices and decisions did you make last year, last month, last week, and yesterday? The most important question of all though is what you are going to choose to think about and decide today. As Jimmy Buffet once said, 'Indecision may or may not be my problem.'

Here is a great tip for you: the best way for you to make choices and decisions is to focus on your purpose. Remember we talked about it earlier, you decided your purpose, who you are, what you're about and what it is you really, really want. When those 60,000 thoughts start flying around in your mind, make a decision first thing every morning to only choose to dwell on those thoughts and images which will take you closer to your purpose and your goals. Choose to only think about those thoughts that can help you, empower you and move you closer to what it is you want. Make a decision to let all of the other unimportant negative stuff go, just let it go.

"If you limit your choices only to what seems possible or reasonable, you disconnect yourself from what you truly want, and all that is left is a compromise."

Robert Fritz

Chapter 8

Use your six gifts

"We are all born with wonderful gifts. We use these gifts to express ourselves, to amuse, to strengthen, and to communicate. We begin as children to explore and develop our talents, often unaware that we are unique, that not everyone can do what we're doing!"

Lynn Johnston

As human beings we are all hard-wired to experience the world around us through our five senses of sight, sound, smell, taste and touch. Information is presented to us through these senses from the outside world and then based on our beliefs and values we act on what we see, hear, smell, taste or touch. Of course in terms of choice and decision two of the most significant factors affecting most of us are what we see and what we hear. We consciously hear something from listening to our spouse, a friend, colleague, the television or radio and we choose whether to give it meaning in our lives and then regardless of whether that meaning is positive or negative we immediately turn it over to our subconscious mind. Many of the 60,000 thoughts we experience each day are triggered by one of the five senses and once many are accepted, whether positive or negative, without any further thought or analysis, they are handed over to the subconscious. One of my mentors, Bob Proctor, a brilliant speaker, author and teacher reminded me about the many other incredible gifts we all have that most of us take for granted and never exercise.

Bob Proctor taught me that living our lives purely through the faculty of our five senses may well sound fine but it's not always the best use of our minds. You see, the conscious mind is the thinking mind. It's the part of the mind that knows you are reading this and knows that you know you are reading this. It's the here and now part of you that is (or at least can be) totally aware of everything that's going on in the moment.

What are you aware of right now?

Whilst you are reading this if I asked you to turn your attention to your foot and to feel the texture of your sock or shoe on your foot you would have no trouble noticing exactly how it felt. If I asked you to feel the temperature of your foot or the tightness and fit of your shoes your conscious mind can process all of this information very easily. Interestingly though, just a few moments ago you had no real idea what your foot felt like in your sock or shoe at that moment, because you gave it no conscious attention. If I asked you to turn your attention to your breathing and notice the depth, the pace, the feeling of your chest moving in and out, the softness and temperature of your breath on each nostril, again your conscious mind can think about all of this easily. The point is there are literally millions and millions of things we can be aware of at any moment in time if we made a choice and decision to become aware of them. The reality, however, is that we would never do such a thing, because so much of it is so trivial and insignificant to us that it would be pointless.

What's more important though is that most of it is taken care of by our subconscious mind, so we never have to concern ourselves with them. Remember, it's our subconscious that is responsible for all of our habits so we can carry on sleepwalking, on autopilot. Our subconscious mind is the feeling part of our mind, so we have to be really careful about what we turn over to it from our conscious mind through dwelling on a negative thought or issue for too long. The ancient Greeks would refer to the subconscious mind as our heart of hearts, believing that it was the seat of all of our feelings.

So you see here is how it works: we soak up information through our five senses and consciously evaluate that information before filtering it through to our subconscious. When the information hits our subconscious it's converted into a feeling, we either feel good or bad about what just got through. It's the way we feel that then drives the way we behave. If we feel bad we act in a way that's not conducive to positive actions and results, if we feel good then our behaviour and results tend to show up as positive. Now I know I've radically simplified the whole process; that is because I believe it doesn't have to be complex. It's an established scientific fact that it's our thoughts that generate our feelings, it's our feelings that cause us to act and behave the way we do and it's our actions that produce our results. So if you want to know what you were thinking about 10 years ago look at your results today.

The problem is because it's so simple most people don't buy it. We like to make things complicated; if it's that simple how could it possible work? It's probably the greatest and simplest truth you are ever going to hear though: your thoughts cause your feelings, your feelings drive your behaviour and it's your behaviour that causes your results. It's classic cause and effect, one of the greatest universal laws: for every effect there is a cause; for every result there is a reason.

Now the reality is, many people focus on the result and see it as the cause rather than the effect. Many people see their results as a reflection of their potential when it should never be that way. Our current results are only ever a reflection of our past. If you want to change your results you have to go back to the cause and the cause is what you are thinking about now. If you want to change your results and you go back to the cause then you must not make the mistake of repeatedly asking yourself WHY? Don't go back to cause and keep asking why you were thinking the way you thought for the results to turn out the way they did. For the most part it doesn't matter, it's irrelevant and insignificant.

The real question you need to ask yourself to change the result is WHAT? What is it you need to think about and visualise now and how do you think about it. Remember your thoughts drive your feelings so don't ask why; if you ask why, you get negative responses and you feel negative, if you ask what, you focus on the positive and therefore feel positive.

Here is the HOW part. As well as five incredible gifts of sight, sound, smell, taste and touch, Bob Proctor has achieved enormous global success by reminding us that we each have access to six other extremely precious gifts that we rarely think about. If we think about them we take them for granted and if we don't we find ourselves ill equipped to use them. These gifts are:

1. **Perception** – Have you ever stopped for a moment to think about the way you see things? You see, many of us grow up thinking about the world in a certain way even though that way isn't necessarily true. It's often a perception of the world and our place in it that we learned from our parents. Imagine the difference in the following two mindsets: Mindset one sees the world as a bad place full of lack and limitation with everybody only caring about themselves and looking for every opportunity to 'screw' the other person. Mindset two on the other hand sees a world of opportunity and possibility where they absolutely know and believe that the universe is plentiful and that they can have whatever they want and the only key to their success or failure is them, no one or nothing else but them.

"When you change the way you look at things the things you look at change."

Dr Wayne Dyer

Imagine a person looking for a relationship whose perception is that all members of the opposite sex are bad people and only care about themselves, compared to the seeker who sees a world where people on the whole are caring, sensitive and genuine and they just know that their perfect partner is out there waiting for them. Think about the person working for the company that has a perception that you can only get promoted if your face fits, compared to the person who is energised by the fact that they know that anyone can reach the top if they really want it.

Most people believe that perception is reality, meaning that what they see and what they believe is fact, it's the way it is, but that's just not true. Perception is not reality, it's perceived reality; it's what we believe to be true. As I mentioned earlier, Dr Wayne Dyer said, 'When you change the way you look at things the things you look at change.' Think about that for a moment: if you have spent your whole life seeing the world as a place of lack and limitation where only the strong survive and those who are supremely intelligent do well, change that to the complete opposite and imagine how you will begin to fly.

The fact is we all have the facility and power of perception; we can choose to change the way we look at anything in a heartbeat. What's really helpful though is when you begin to fall in love with your life, when you just accept yourself and your life as unique and special with infinite potential. Let's say you want to be financially free or independent but your perception is that money is evil and that everyone with money is a liar and a cheat. Let's say you want to lose weight but your perception is that people in your family can never control their weight or that losing weight equals pain; how do you think you will move on?

Once again it comes down to choice and decision: you have to choose how you want to see the world and the opportunities within it and then you have to decide. The brilliant fact is that we have the power of perception, even though we may have looked at a certain thing in the same way for many years, we can change. The easiest way to do this is to write down the limiting perception and then cross it out and write down the exact opposite perception and read it several times each day. Write it on a small piece of card that you can easily carry around in your wallet or purse and take it out and read it aloud to yourself as many times as you can each day.

I remember growing up in a situation where my parents didn't have much money at all. At its worst I remember coming home from school many afternoons to find my mother upset and crying, searching behind the sofas to see if she could find loose change to be able to go to the shops to buy food to feed us. For a short spell my perception was that was how people like us were supposed to live, but it didn't last for too long; I quickly changed to the view that we were as good as anyone else and we could have whatever we wanted. I learned to change my perception to one where I believed that I could be, do or have anything I wanted in my life despite my parents' 'bad luck'. How did I do that? Simple really, I just chose to think that I could have anything I wanted and I kept telling myself the same thing over and over again. It's called self talk.

We have a very special, very unique gift of perception and if you invest just a little time and effort to change the way you are looking at the world and your life or any situation I can promise you that the things you are looking at will change.

Can you imagine a business succeeding if the executive team's perception was that everyone else's products were better than theirs and that there was just no place for them in the market? Can you imagine any of the successful people who ever walked this earth having a perception that success was always for the other person and never for them. Look at the way you are looking at the world and your life and think about the perceptions you need to change.

2. **Imagination** – Possibly the most priceless of human gifts is the imagination. Einstein himself said that imagination is more powerful than knowledge. It's also a fact that the subconscious finds it extremely difficult and sometimes even impossible to tell the difference between imagination and reality. If I were to ask you to go sit in a quiet room, turn all of the lights off and close your eyes for a moment to imagine the following scenario:

You are walking home from a friend's house late at night and it's cold, dark and you can hear footsteps behind you. There is no one else on the street except you and the footsteps behind you. As you turn each corner the footsteps turn with you getting closer and louder; you turn very slightly to see if you can catch a glimpse of the person behind you and for a brief second you see what looks like a sharp shiny metal object in someone's hand... You tell yourself you are being followed and the person is carrying a knife. How does that make you feel? Most of us can have such a visual image make our heart beat faster and the palms of our hands sweaty and overall leave us feeling very nervous, but none of it is real.

Many people use their imagination in a negative way; when they have a goal or a dream they immediately kill it stone dead by imagining everything that could possibly go wrong. They imagine all of the obstacles, all of the difficulties and all of the pain of things not going they way they want them to.

The fact is that for anything to happen in the real world it firstly has to happen in the imaginary world. Remember to just take a look around you wherever you are reading this right now and think about how absolutely everything once started with someone creating a picture in their mind. Imagination is simply the process of creating a picture in your mind and the reality is we all have that ability; however similar to our power of perception, it's an intellectual faculty that most of us either take for granted or use in a negative way. There is no question that we all have a vivid imagination it's just a case of whether we choose to use it and if we do, in what context and for what purpose. As a practising hypnotherapist one of the techniques I use every single time with my patients to instigate change is imagination, their own imagination. Through the power of suggestion I get them to see themselves at their ideal weight, or at a dinner party where someone offers them a cigarette and they decline, or relaxing calmly and comfortably on an aeroplane. When I'm using hypnosis with people who have a physical symptom, I use a technique called the healing white light whereby the patient imagines a warm, soothing healing white light flowing through their body healing the ailment. The use of imagination in or out of hypnosis is incredibly powerful, yet not too many of us consciously choose to tap in to such a precious gift.

Every successful organisation on this planet, every successful person who has ever walked this earth has achieved success through the power of their own imagination. Nothing on this planet that is man-made did not start in the imagination. There is no secret, it's a simple straightforward process; all you need to do is to write down what it is that you want, I mean really want, and then to see yourself already having it.

Imagination is everything!

The challenge is to use your imagination as frequently and with as much colour, clarity and feeling as you can muster. I refer to it as a challenge because when most people make the conscious decision to try it for the first time they give up quickly. The reason they give up quickly is because the image isn't always as clear as they would wish or expect it to be or worse still if the goal didn't materialise the very next day they would say it didn't work and move on, discrediting imagination.

The reason imagination is so powerful and critical to success is as I have already explained, but let me clarify: we choose our thoughts with our conscious mind, this is our thinking mind in which we can choose to accept or reject any thought that comes to us and through it we can create ideas.

Once we have consciously accepted a thought we turn it over to our subconscious mind. Now our subconscious mind has no ability to reject this thought once it's handed over, that is the role of the conscious. The subconscious mind is our emotional mind, it the part of the mind we feel with and as we feel we send our body into an altered state of vibration. We either feel good or bad about the thought. As we begin to feel a certain way that's when we start to act. If we feel good we act in a positive way, if we feel bad we act in a negative way. That's where our imagination has such a vital role to play. If we use our imagination to make that thought feel as positive as possible by visualising the goal and all of the goodness attached to it we can make ourselves feel great. If we feel great, we act great.

It's our actions and behaviour that determines our results. If you are wondering why you don't get the results you want in your life, think about the way you have been feeling and how you have used your imagination. Imagination has a huge, huge role to play; how do you use yours?

3. **Will** – Another of our fine intellectual faculties is our will. By this I do not mean willpower, I mean our ability to focus, our ability to have a goal and to concentrate on that goal and to focus on it at the exclusion of all other distractions. I mean our sense of purposefulness and clarity that allows us the concentration and determination to achieve whatever it is we set out to achieve. We all have a strong will and we have all used it many, many times as children and as we were growing up. Just like our imagination as children, our will was very prominent in our lives, but as we grew up many of us used these gifts less and less, to the point where just like any muscle if you don't use it often enough it becomes weak. It's still there though and it's waiting and longing to be used, all you have to do is exercise it like you would a muscle in the gym.

We all know what is possible for us when we really set our minds on something, as we have all been there as children and adults; the issue is that this is another of our intellectual gifts that we forget about and take for granted. I believe that the reason for this is the absence of passion and clarity. You see, if we either don't really know what we want or we do know but we are not passionate enough about what we want, then it's unlikely that we will turn to the power of our will often. The wonderful thing about the gift of will, just like imagination and perception, is that none of these gifts are dependent upon a certain level of intelligence, maturity or wealth. It doesn't matter who you are, where you are or what you have achieved or not achieved in your life, you can tap into your will in a heartbeat. To focus and concentrate on what it is you want at the exclusion of everything else the only prerequisite is that you have to be clear about what it is you want and you have to really want it.

Even the good old classics like giving up smoking or losing weight which so many people find impossible only seem impossible, because often the person isn't crystal clear about why they want to give up smoking or lose weight and that lack of clarity brings doubt, fear and confusion rather than passion. If there is something that you really, really, really wish to be, do or have, then I'm here to tell you that you have the will to make the possibility possible.

I have used my will to good effect many, many times in my life both in a professional and personal context. I have had the will to turn a business completely around and succeeded and I have had the will to lose weight and improve my health, to stop smoking, to find fulfilling work, to become financially independent, to massively improve my self worth, to grow and excel on all levels as a father, son and husband and I still have a lot to learn and do but am succeeding.

4. Memory – Let us not forget about our amazing memories. Most people I meet tend to talk about what a terrible memory they have especially as they start to get a little older. The fact is that within our subconscious mind we have a vast library of everything that has ever happened to us, good, bad and indifferent. However, just like perception, imagination and will, our memory isn't something we think about very often and whenever we are forced to we invariably criticise it. I have fallen into the same trap in the past myself as I have with all of these faculties. I remember when I was revising for my hypnotherapy exam and I realised I had to remember a long list of hypnotic phenomena with names, dates and full descriptions. I froze, terrified and helpless, immediately telling myself how it was impossible because I had such a poor memory. To make matters worse, I didn't just tell myself, I complained about it to others at every opportunity. It was only my tutor who thankfully set me straight on this.

During a tutorial she asked me how my revision was going for the exam and I told her how terrible I felt about this list I had to remember and what an awful memory I had and how it seemed impossible. Well, she instantly corrected me by reminding me that if that was what I kept telling myself I would find it easy to prove myself right, and what's more it was a glaring lie because I had a brilliant memory, I just didn't know how to use it properly. At this point she taught me a couple of simple techniques to remember the list easily and in order. I went off to practise and within a couple of hours I could easily recall the list without any difficulty.

Once again my memory was just like any other muscle in my body although it was one I hadn't actively practised using in a positive way and it was therefore weak. The reason our memories are such powerful gifts is that they contain such precious positive information, that when recalled with even only a small degree of clarity can change our entire emotional and physiological state. I believe that most of us have positive memories. Most of us can think back to a time when we felt love, either loved by someone or loving someone. Most of us can think of a happy time, a time when life felt good or at the very least better than it may feel now. Most of us have achieved something in life even if it's learning to ride a bike, or getting a job. Many of us have a whole wealth of good memories of times, things and events that made us happy, excited, joyful, curious, energised, confident, playful, determined, passionate. The problem is though that many of us choose to spend a disproportionate amount of time recalling negative memories. We think about all of the bad things that ever happened to us, things that people said or did to us, relationships and jobs that we lost or went wrong, all of the obstacles, all of the failures, and all of the pain we went through.

We then take those nasty negative memories and play them again over and over in our minds like a bad movie until we relive the experience convincing ourselves how bad or unlucky we are and why we can never have the level of success we want.

It doesn't have to be that way though as you can see, we can use those empowering memories to good effect; all we have to do is take the time to tune into them and hold them with our will. Think and recall the good times, all of the great things that you have experienced so far in your life, and when you have that image in your mind make it as bright and as colourful and as loud as possible. See what you saw back then, feel exactly what you felt and even hear what you heard, relive the positive memories and tap into how those times made you feel. Remember your first kiss, passing your driving test, succeeding at an interview, sunbathing on a beach, walking in the woods, remember anything and everything that makes you feel good and empowers you.

5. **Reason** – Reason is our ability to think for ourselves; it's our ability to generate and formulate ideas, to construct arguments and analyse. It is through this wonderful gift that we can receive information from any one of the five senses or any other source, to consider it carefully and to then decide whether we wish to accept, reject or even neglect any thought which comes to us. It is through reason that we accept an idea and

turn it over to the subconscious mind. It's the ability to reason that enables us to think and make choices and decisions. When a thought or an idea comes to mind your reasoning factor allows you to ask yourself questions about the thought such as:

Will this bring me pain or pleasure?

Will this move me in the direction of my goal?

How will this make me feel?

Will this improve the quality of my life – will this help or hinder me?

Will this lead to certainty or uncertainty?

Will this lead to growth or take me backwards?

What does this mean to me right now?

How will this contribute to the results I get in my life?

Is this good or bad?

Is this right or wrong?

You see, it's our ability to think, evaluate, to ask ourselves questions, to perceive, imagine and use our will that sets us apart from every other species on the planet. The real question is how conscious and focused are we on the power of reason and the opportunities and possibilities it can create for us. How do you think? What do you think? What questions do you ask yourself and what do you allow to enter your subconscious mind?

6. Intuition – The dictionary definition of intuition is 'a keen and quick insight'. It is derived from the Latin word 'intueri' which means 'to see within'. It is a means of knowing, or sensing the truth without any explanation. Many of us call this our gut instinct whereby we do not believe ourselves to be spiritual but somehow we get a strong feeling from somewhere about something that we just cannot explain. Often this can be really frustrating when we seem to get a message from somewhere but do not get any logical reasoning along with it.

Everyone is apparently somewhat psychic, but many people simply have weak psychic muscles. Learning to listen to your inner voice can strengthen this muscle, and like any other muscle the more you use it the stronger it gets. The problem is many people choose to ignore their gut instincts when often it is the quickest, clearest and most effective way to a positive solution, outcome or idea.

Intuition is what you use to find the purpose of your life, to tune into your passion and your place in the world. Once you awaken your inner guide by unlocking the wisdom of your subconscious mind, you know exactly what to do. Intuition is the ability to get a sense, vision or feeling about someone or something. Intuition communicates with us through our feelings and emotions. It usually does not speak to us in clear language. We are all born with intuition and use it well and often as children, but as we grow older and our rational and reasonable mind develops, we lose touch with this incredible gift. The good news is that the brightness of our intuition can be restored with effort and practice

The easiest method is focus. By focusing on an object, relaxing, and taking deep breaths, we can retrain our minds to let our intuition surface. When we concentrate on a single object, once a day, everyday, and block out our rational mind, we begin the journey to get back in touch with our intuition. First of all, get comfortable, sit down, relax and take 3–4 deep breaths. Look at an object in the room, focus, concentrate, block everything else out. Do that for at least 5 minutes. Now, close you eyes and think about everything that comes to your mind.

When you listen to your intuition it connects you with a far greater knowledge. Accessing your intuition through your subconscious mind can provide a wonderful feeling of peace in the midst of chaos, bring you to harmony, help you release negativity, and give you confidence to take action and prepare for change in your life. It also can be a valuable guide as you take steps to create your dreams. Don't be so quick to dismiss your intuition.

Remember those times when you couldn't stop thinking about someone during the day, maybe someone you hadn't seen for a long time but for some strange reason their name or face just popped into your mind.

Then that very same evening whilst you were at home relaxing the phone rang, you answered it and strangely it was the very same person you had been thinking about all day long. Or it may not have been the phone call, you may have bumped into them in a shop or a car park having not seen them for months or even years when suddenly you started thinking about them and there they were. Things happen that we sometimes just can't readily explain, those feelings or voices, and sometimes it's worth listening and taking them seriously.

The only way you will ever get off of the treadmill and make sure you stay off is to use these six miraculous gifts. So hold them close and value them as priceless, because they are to you. Make sure you start exercising them so they grow strong, effective and efficient and help you to realise your full and maximum potential in all that you do.

Think as often as you can about these six intellectual gifts you have been given to develop these thoughts, experiences and ideas to help you to get off the treadmill and lead the life of your dreams.

"The only real valuable thing is intuition."

Albert Einstein

Chapter 9

Put your health first

*"Of all the self-fulfilling prophecies in our culture,
the assumption that aging means decline and poor
health is probably the deadliest."*

Marilyn Ferguson

You can get off the treadmill and decide your purpose, you can build the most exciting, colourful and powerful vision known to man, but none of it is any use to you if you don't have your health. The whole point of getting off the treadmill and building the life of your dreams so that you can have more, be more and do more, is that you can enjoy it. To enjoy anything wouldn't it be a great idea to experience that enjoyment through the luxury of a healthy body and mind. Doesn't it make sense that your absolute number one all consuming priority should be your health. Not just the health of your physical body but the health of your mind and your spirit too.

Isn't it true that most people know exactly what is required to lead a healthy life, but that even those people who know absolutely what to do, show little or no sign of having this knowledge through their behaviour. Isn't it true that some of the most intelligent, sensible, responsible people you know, who know exactly what is required of them to lead a long and healthy life go out there into the world and do the exact opposite of what they know they should do.

Even though people have access to knowledge and information it doesn't always and in many cases very rarely alters their behaviour with regard to their health. You see, most of our waking lives are lived through habit; we go to bed at the same time each night, wake up at the same time each morning, use the same toothpaste and soap, eat the same cereal, wear the same type of clothes, drive the same route to work, do largely the same things in the same way each day, eating the same foods, having the same mannerisms and even thinking the same thoughts. Our lives are dominated by habit largely because we just live our lives through our five senses never giving too much thought to our six intellectual faculties and how we have the absolute power to change any aspect of our lives in a heartbeat. So when it comes to smoking, we smoke because we have trained our subconscious to accept that as perfectly acceptable behaviour even though our conscious mind knows it's crazy. At some point in the past we used our will to accept smoking as acceptable and therefore our subconscious had no choice but to accept that too. When something becomes such a strong habit we continue to perform the habit regardless of the consequences. The problem is that when we do finally one day make a decision to stop smoking and lead a more healthy life we find it extremely difficult because no one has told the subconscious.

It's not just smoking, it's the same with drinking excessive amounts of alcohol each day or overeating all of the wrong foods or maybe even just very rarely, if ever, eating the right foods. It also becomes a habit for most people to drink very little water each day.

Intellectual understanding isn't enough

If you stopped anyone in the street and asked them how many glasses of water they should be drinking each day the vast majority would be able to tell you the answer of eight. Equally though if you asked those same people who got the question right again the majority will tell you they drink far less than eight glasses of water each day, with many drinking no water at all during a typical day. So my point is this, it isn't so much about education because most people know. I believe most people know the dangers of smoking, excessive alcohol consumption, not drinking enough water, not eating enough healthy food and not exercising but that knowledge makes little difference to their behaviour.

The reality is all we have to do is make a choice and a decision. We must choose to live long healthy lives and then act on it. So when we are inundated with those 60,000 thoughts each day we need to think about which of them contribute to our goal of a long, healthy happy life and quickly discard those that are not in harmony with that goal. Good health is about living a conscious life; it's about not just knowing but about doing. It's about understanding who you truly are, falling in love with your life and having respect for your body. It's about awareness, your awareness of your six intellectual gifts and your awareness of how you can use them to get whatever it is you want, including great health. If you hold the perception that everyone gets sick as they get older and there is nothing you can do about it, change your perception because it is not even close to reality. If you hold the perception that your smoking, drinking, or overeating won't harm you because that only happens to other people, change your perception because it is a lie. If your perception is that you have no control or choice because that's just the 'way you are' or 'it's your parents fault' then change it because it's a lie.

If you have been using your intellectual faculty of reason to tell yourself that you don't have a problem and it'll be ok, then think again because it won't. Use your gift of reason and perception to think about all of the wonderful benefits of leading a long, happy healthy life. Use reason to think about all of the opportunities and possibilities great health can afford you. Use reason to acknowledge how special and unique you really are and how vital it is that you look after your body especially as you only ever get the one. If you have used reason to give you an excuse to smoke because you are bored, lonely, sad, hurting, worried, anxious, or scared, then get clear on your purpose and use your imagination to get you back on track. Remember the piece of research that I referred to in a previous chapter whereby the secret to the longevity of the centenarians studied was purpose and exercise. Think about those two things: Are you really clear on your purpose? Do you exercise?

Firstly, think about purpose, and know that when you get really crystal clear on why you do what you do and where you are heading there is no room for ill health. It's the absence and lack of clarity of purpose that is often the cause of the problem so do whatever it takes to understand and rekindle your passion and make a decision to live a healthy life. Don't ignore your health, don't turn your back on it, and don't pretend it's not your responsibility or that everything will turn out just fine. Use your gifts and protect your health today, don't even wait until tomorrow, do it today.

When I used to smoke, overeat and drink too much and made a decision to change I always said, I will do it tomorrow, or Monday morning, or on the first of the month, or my birthday, or New Year's Day. The old saying that you have heard and overused yourself, 'tomorrow never comes' is desperately true… So do it today. Tomorrow truly never comes.

So the terms for physical health and longevity are as you know them already but for the avoidance of doubt here they are again:

- Decide your purpose, get clear on it and if you don't have one then decide one.

- Exercise. That doesn't mean you have to go to the gym (although that would be helpful), just stay active, and keep moving.

- Don't smoke and if you do quit today – stop making excuses, go to the cancer ward of a hospital if you have to or spend Sunday morning visiting your local cemetery or close your eyes and visualise yourself telling the people you love most that you are dying from cancer.

- Eat well, plenty of fruit and vegetables and cut out the bad fats.

- Sleep well.

- Learn to relax.

- Learn to breathe properly.

- Drink plenty of water.

- Have fun and laugh lots.

Calm down

As well as substantially limiting the number of toxins you put into your body, avoid stress. Stress like smoking is another major contributor to illness and disease. The way to avoid stress is to live consciously, become aware of what you are thinking at any moment and then become very clear about how those thoughts are making you feel. The antidote to stress is to remember the cycle: your thoughts cause your feelings which cause your behaviour and your behaviour can then drive more negative thoughts and bad feelings, fuelling the vicious loop. So monitor your thoughts and change them at will to change your feelings.

A lot of stress is caused by doubt, fear and confusion and can be avoided and managed if you get crystal clear on what it is you want. Get clear on what you really, really want and then remember that we think in pictures so use your gift of imagination to bring that picture up on the screen of your mind and use your will to hold it at the exclusion of all other distractions. Be aware that a lot of times stress comes down to us simply not giving our minds something better to do, so use your gift of reason and give it something better to do.

Also make a point each day to calm down; you don't necessarily have to slow down (although that would be helpful too) but it is essential that you calm down and breathe. It's scientifically impossible to be able to hold two states at the same time, so in other words you can't be tense and relaxed in the same moment so stay focused and intent on staying relaxed. The best way to relax is to be conscious of your breathing and take long, slow deep breaths being aware of your breathing and the feeling of the breath through your body and mind.

Stop worrying by giving your mind something better to think about. If you are worried about something then take some time out, write down the specific worry and then list all of the worst things that could happen if your worry were to become realised. Once you have your list of outcomes then write down a list of all the possible solutions to the worry and once you are satisfied that you have exhausted the list of possibilities, continue to sit quietly with your list and ask yourself which solution you like best. Don't stop there: ask yourself which solution you are prepared to act on.

If you are crystal clear in your own mind that there is absolutely no solution to the worry then you have no choice but to just let it go and plan for the consequences of the outcome. Stress can affect every part of the body in so many different ways:

1. **The Brain** – Stress begins in the brain through an increase in neurochemicals causing intense alertness which sometimes causes us to find it difficult to relax or even sleep at night. If high stress levels are pro-

longed then we can feel the physical effects in the form of tension headaches, irritability, aggression, inability to concentrate and memory loss. Excessive prolonged stress can also cause depression. Chronic stress over long periods can overload the brain with powerful hormones which over a period of time damages and kills brain cells.

2. **The Ears** – The increase in hormones triggered by stress improves our hearing to help us react to danger and this isn't always a good thing as research shows that even moderate noise elevates heart-damaging stress hormones. Research has also shown that a lot of small noisy stressors added together such as car horns, ringing telephones and loud people can be more dangerous to the body than one major stressful event.

3. **The Lungs** – Part of the body's fight or flight response when we are seriously stressed is to hyperventilate. Fight or flight is a built in mechanism that is triggered through stress to increase oxygen into our bloodstream so we can run for cover. Unfortunately such a quick succession of breaths can cause dizziness and sharp pains in the diaphragm. Severe stress can aggravate asthma and other dangerous respiratory conditions.

4. **The Eyes** – The surge of adrenaline from stress dilates the eyes improving vision, although it can easily trigger eye ticks because eye muscles become fatigued.

5. **The Mouth** – Dry mouth and bad breath are common when affected by stress. Prolonged stress can result in some people clenching their jaws or grinding their teeth.

6. **The Hair** – Hair is often the first to suffer. Stress is known to cause the burning of nutrients which can lead to dull hair and premature greying. Chronic stress can cause the autoimmune system to attack hair follicles, causing hair loss.

7. **The Heart** – Stress can cause your heart to pump fast and hard resulting in blood pressure rising as the body produces the hormone epinephrine as well as the hormone cortisol. This can cause heart palpitations and chest pains.

8. **Immune System** – Severe and constant stress lowers the white blood cell count, leaving us more open to disease and stifling the body's ability to heal itself.

9. **Joints, Muscles and Bones** – During stress, our brain sends messages to the muscles, tightening them and preparing them for action. Chronic stress can aggravate rheumatoid arthritis, cause sore muscles and make us prone to sprains.

10. **Skin** – The release of hormones while under stress can cause acne and a variety of rashes. Extreme stress can trigger hives and any skin condition can be made worse through stress.

11. **Digestive System** – Blood flows away from the digestive tract under stress which slows digestion, often resulting in indigestion, diarrhoea, constipation, incontinence and colon spasm. Stress increases acid production, aggravating ulcers. It is also linked to colitis and irritable bowel syndrome, a painful and sometimes debilitating disorder.

I could go on and on and on...

Don't forget to breathe!

It was only after spending 30 years or so on the planet breathing that I learned that I and probably 99 per cent of my fellow human beings weren't breathing properly. Breathing, like using the mind, seemed to be a natural process, something we were just born to do and so it required little training. Breathing is central to life and is a basic animal instinct. In humans it is also central to speech, singing, laughing, sighing and crying. Without balance in breathing the whole being is affected. Breathing is the process by which a balance between oxygen and carbon dioxide is maintained.

If this balance is disturbed by a lack of oxygen or by a lack of carbon dioxide, through hyperventilation, physical symptoms can result. We talked about stress earlier and it's a fact that proper deep considered breathing can be hugely beneficial in avoiding and managing stress, yet none of us are taught how to do it properly. Everyone knows that breathing is essential to life. Life begins when we inhale our first breath and ends when we exhale our last breath.

Breathing affects virtually every part of the body. It oxygenates the body and revitalises organs, cells and tissues. Breathing properly can help:

- Fuel energy production,

- Improve focus and concentration,

- Eliminate toxins,

- Strengthen the immune system,

- Improve bowel function,

- Reduce stress, tension and anxiety,

- Increase feelings of calmness and relaxation,

- Lower blood pressure,

- Increase metabolism, aiding in digestion and weight loss.

On the other hand, not breathing correctly can cause problems for a number of systems in the body, including the immune, circulatory, endocrine and nervous systems. Improper breathing can produce a variety of symptoms including:

- Mental fog,

- Dizziness,

- Numbness,

- Anxiety,

- Chest pain,

- Digestive problems,

- Irritable bowel,

- Neck and shoulder pain.

So having told you that most of us haven't been taught how to breathe properly here is a simple exercise to teach you how to do exactly that:

1. Stand straight, sit upright or lie down.

2. Place your hands on your stomach.

3. Breathe in through your nose, counting to five. Picture a balloon in your stomach that you're inflating with the air you are inhaling. Your hands should rise as your stomach fills with air.

4. Hold your breath for a few seconds.

5. Exhale slowly through your mouth, counting to four. Picture letting the air out of the balloon in your stomach. Your hands should go down as your stomach deflates.

The fact is stress is a silent killer; it's one of those menaces that creep up on you without you knowing and the fact is that whilst it is something that most people talk about openly and blame for everything, most people don't really know they are suffering from stress. The reality is, stress is inevitable, it's part of daily life, and whilst it's not something you can readily avoid, it is something you can prepare for. Prepare for the effects of stress and the impact it can have on your health by not just knowing, but by doing, by preparing.

I want you to take these pages as an instruction to stop knowing and start doing. Don't wait until it's too late; don't wait until you are too ill to do anything about it and then say to yourself I knew exactly what to do I only wish I'd done it. It will be too late, so do it now. You have all the tools you need; all you have to do is use them. The next chapter offers you the best means you will ever find of managing stress.

"A wise man should consider that health is the greatest of human blessings, and learn how by his own thought to derive benefit from his illnesses."

Hippocrates

Chapter 10

Use your mind, practise self hypnosis

"You can chain me, you can torture me, you can even destroy this body, but you will never imprison my mind."

Mahatma Ghandi

As a fully trained and qualified hypnotherapist, having travelled all over the world to seminars and workshops on personal development, having read hundreds of books and listened to many, many CDs, having watched DVD after DVD on the subject of fulfilment and success, I can distil everything I've learned into just one simple secret.

My findings point to the reality that there is only one tool available to each and every person on this planet to enable them to have whatever it is they want, be that great health, financial abundance, loving relationships, fulfilling work, happiness or peace of mind. That tool lies in each of us, it doesn't cost a penny to own and nobody can ever take it away from us. It's more than a tool though, it's a gift, the gift of all gifts because through it you can live the life of your dreams once you know how to use it. There is a challenge though, because as it is given to you at birth it comes without instructions and therefore many of us spend the majority of our lives desperately trying to work out how to use it. Some of us though, believe it or not, are oblivious to the fact that it serves a purpose let alone being the most powerful and incredible of all gifts.

Some of the best brains on earth have been studying the gift since the beginning of recorded time and much progress has been made; however, despite the intellect, intense curiosity and studies of many of these seekers, no one has yet come up with all of the answers.

Scientists, psychiatrists, doctors, philosophers, psychotherapists, leaders and enthusiasts from all walks of life have committed a lifetime of study to learn the secrets of the gift and have so far all come to only one common conclusion. That conclusion is this: the only resource we will ever need regardless of who we are, where we are, our background, culture, education, colour, intellect or environment, is our mind. **We literally become what we think about the most. The gift is the mind – it is all we will ever need to succeed or fail.**

Everything I have studied, every book, every seminar, every CD, every DVD, every workshop, every piece of research all pointed to the same gift. **The gift is our mind!**

Yet wherever you choose to go anywhere in the world you will find millions, upon millions, upon millions of people looking for success outside of themselves. There are countless people who have little or no knowledge that they can be, do or have whatever it is they want if they learn how to use their mind properly. So many people are searching for pills, potions, gadgets and gurus to give them what they crave more than anything on earth: great health, great wealth, great peace and great happiness. The difficulty and sad reality is that this has become a global issue because as we have continued the journey from birth, to childhood, to adolescence, to adulthood no one has told us about the power of the mind, our intellectual faculties, or even our two levels of mind as the conscious and subconscious. These are things we have had to learn the hard way. I guess we would expect these things to have been properly explained to us by our parents, our grandparents and school teachers and whilst some of us have been lucky and have had parents or teachers who understood the importance of this knowledge and shared it with us, for the most part many of us grew up in ignorance.

What's worse is that because we have lived and experienced life the hard way, when many of us do eventually find out about the gift, the simplicity of its existence and use is just too much for us to take in so we choose to dismiss its power and carry on as we were. Of course, often this choice isn't highly conscious because it's largely the fact that we have been living life and thinking through habit for so long, that the perception is that it would take far too much effort to explore another possibility or another way of thinking. Have you ever stopped for a moment to think about how we learn about the mind and how this powerful device works?

When I was growing up I don't ever remember anyone sitting me down and explaining to me that I had two levels of mind, the conscious and subconscious, and how these levels worked. I don't recall lessons specifically devoted to the vastness of my intellectual faculties. No one told me about perception, imagination, will, reason, intuition and memory. I guess I kind of stumbled across these things in one form or another as I got older, but I certainly never studied them; I most definitely never had it explained to me that these gifts could shape my entire world and life on this planet.

I remember learning and studying things like maths, English, art, drama, science, geography, history and languages. I even remember doing a bit of biology and learning a small amount about the brain, but no one ever talked about the mind, my mind. It took me many years to understand that the only reason this was the case was that no one seemed to really know how the mind worked and if they did it certainly wasn't something that was spoken about. I guess the function of the mind was a bit like breathing: it was natural, something we all did and didn't really need to understand it, so we took it for granted and just got on with it.

Now I've explained the importance of breathing properly and how to do it let's move on to talk about the mind. As I've said we covered parts of the mind in several places throughout the book, but I'd like to capture it like this for you to really get it. We each have one mind but two levels within it. The conscious mind is the thinking mind, the rational, analytical, problem solving, choosing, decision making tool. We each have around 60,000 thoughts each day entering our conscious mind, but it's still far more powerful than that. If we really turned it on and were totally conscious of every single aspect of our environment at any moment in time we could be aware of billions of pieces of information. Analogies are always being made to the conscious mind being like a supercomputer but the reality is that the conscious and subconscious combined would out perform any computer which could ever be created. Nothing could ever get close.

With the conscious mind we think and create thought and we can choose to accept, reject or just neglect any thought that comes to us. We can experience the world through our five senses with the conscious mind interpreting the information flowing to us. We can perceive the world and any aspect of it in any way we choose through our conscious mind and we can change that perception in an instant. We can imagine the world and any aspect of it, ourselves and anything we choose to be, have or do in any way, shape or form that may take our fancy, all through the conscious mind. We can create heaven or hell through our imagination alone. We can create lack and limitation or total abundance. We can create health or sickness, fear or love, pain or pleasure, success or failure. We can create a product or service that can literally change the face and future of the world forever.

It's with our conscious mind that we can reason. We can choose to think about anything we want at any time and change it in an instant. No one can force us to think about something we choose not to think about. We can use our conscious mind to tap into our subconscious and relive any memory we choose to experience again. We can choose to remember the good times or the bad, the happy times or sad times, our successes or failures. Each of these choices of memory is activated by the conscious mind. When we have an idea, or a goal or an image through our conscious mind we can hold it with our will. We can hold that image to focus and concentrate on it at the exclusion of all other distractions; all we have to do is make the conscious decision to use the power. And finally we can tune into our intuition by making a conscious choice to sit quietly for a moment and rest the conscious mind to allow our subconscious to tell us how we truly feel about anything.

Don't take your subconscious mind for granted!

Of course I have only just scratched the surface of the potential of our conscious and subconscious capability. To think about this power even further I would encourage you to simply look around you, have a real close look at the world you are living in and then pause for a moment to think about how it's changed in the last 100 years. Look at what your fellow man has created, both the good and the not so good, with the conscious mind. When you find yourself getting excited about this infinite potential, then think about the analogy of the conscious and subconscious minds being compared to an iceberg. It has been said that the conscious mind is the very tip of the iceberg, that 10 per cent of mass that you can see towering out of the water, and that the subconscious is the 90 per cent of mass sinking deep into the unknown depths of the ocean where nobody ever goes. The subconscious is the level of mind that truly knows and understands who we are and just what we are capable of and that our potential is also infinite. The subconscious contains information relating to everything that has ever happened to us ever since the moment of our birth; every word, every thought, every feeling and every experience are held in this complex warehouse and can be retrieved at will if we make the time and effort to learn how to tune into it.

The subconscious is the part of us responsible for all of our habits, all of our feelings and it even controls all of our bodily functions critical to our survival that we all take for granted. The subconscious in all its powerful glory does not have the ability to reject or accept an idea once it has been turned over to it by the conscious mind. You can, however, communicate directly with it and get it to directly accept a new idea or response to just about anything. For example, as your conscious mind has programmed your subconscious to smoke, overeat or believe you cannot do something, you can communicate directly with it to alter that view or belief.

Changing beliefs and behaviour through hypnosis!

The best way to communicate directly with the subconscious mind is through hypnosis. There is nothing magical or mystical about hypnosis despite what you may have seen on TV or at the theatre. Hypnosis is the only way known to date of quieting the conscious mind to open a dialogue directly with the subconscious. Whilst it may not be the only method of accessing the subconscious, I know from experience that it is extremely powerful as a means of facilitating change. In its simplest form hypnosis is an altered state of awareness, whereby you attain a lovely feeling of pure relaxation to the point where you cut out all, or at least most, of that 'mind chatter' that we all experience so often. It is the 'mind chatter' or 'noise' that so often stops us from achieving permanent change. So many people tell themselves that they are going to stop smoking, lose weight, increase their confidence, stop being phobic or improve their life or performance in some way, only to find that they then sabotage themselves by constantly telling themselves in their minds exactly why they can't have what they want or do what they want. It's that incessant 'noise' from their conscious mind that stops them from achieving their goal.

The problem is that when you have done or experienced the same thing over and over and over again for long periods of time, you create a habit in your subconscious by simply programming it to do whatever it is that you are doing that you find yourself no longer liking. When that happens, suddenly changing your mind and deciding to stop, change, think or behave differently often just doesn't work because the habit is so deeply entrenched in your subconscious that the conscious instruction to stop, change or behave differently just becomes part of the conscious noise. The way to effect proper and permanent change is to stop the noise and reprogramme your subconscious to behave and feel differently.

I find it fascinating that most people only ever consider hypnosis as a last resort. After they have tried every pill, potion, process, technique or guru and have found that they have spent hundreds of pounds or vast amounts of time to find nothing works they turn in desperation to hypnosis. Sadly, this is all too often the case when it should in fact be the first port of call in so many cases. After all, nothing can change you better than you, although such a philosophy seems too simple and 'too good to be true'. Every one of us has experienced hypnosis and many of us experience it many times each day. Here are some examples:

- You drive the same route to work every day and one morning you find that you have reached a point in the journey but perhaps don't recall the last 5 minutes driving to get to that point because you had 'switched off'.

- You are in a meeting at work and drift off in your mind for 5 minutes.

- You are reading a book and suddenly find you have read a paragraph or even a whole page but your mind was elsewhere.

- You are watching the TV or a film and someone asks you a question which you answer but you don't recall answering because you were 'miles away' with the programme or film.

What has happened in each of these cases is that your conscious mind starts a process and then finds that both your conscious and subconscious are so familiar with whatever it is that you are doing that the behaviour is already embedded in your subconscious so your subconscious takes over control and your conscious drifts off elsewhere. You see, once you have trained the subconscious to do something it goes on 'autopilot' and needs little or no help to carry on the behaviour without your full awareness.

Self hypnosis

Having explained that the best known means of communicating with the subconscious mind is through hypnosis, I must also tell you that you can communicate with your very own subconscious mind very easily yourself through self hypnosis. I believe that all hypnosis is self hypnosis and that when you pay for the expertise of a hypnotherapist you are simply being guided into hypnosis but other than guidance you are doing all of the work yourself. Everyone can enter a state of trance and communicate with their deeper selves through self hypnosis and learning to do so is possibly the most valuable gift you could give to yourself and it costs nothing except a little time and commitment.

There are no rules for when or where to start your practice of self hypnosis, both the location and the time should be what suits you best. Some people prefer the morning whilst some prefer the evening and of course some prefer to do it in both the morning and evening. Try both and see what suits you best.

As far as location goes, just make sure you find somewhere where you know you will not be disturbed, somewhere quiet, where you won't hear the phone or you can disconnect it. Where you can lock the door or put up a do not disturb sign so the kids can't get in. Make sure, it's warm, comfortable and quiet. You can do self hypnosis sitting or lying down, again it's entirely up to you, whatever makes you more comfortable. I prefer to sit up to reduce the likelihood of me falling asleep. Once you have found your time and your place, here's what you do:

EXERCISE

- Just sit or lie down in a comfortable position and let your eyes close.

- As your eyes close just let them relax and focus on your breathing, feeling each gentle breath in and each gentle breath out.

- Starting at the tips of your toes just visualise your muscles relaxing as you say the word relax in your mind. Start moving gently up each body part right up to the top of your head, each time visualising the muscle relaxing whilst saying the word relax in your mind.

- As you relax the top of your head then begin to visualise a path way or a set of strong steps.

- Once you have the image of the path or steps begin to count slowly down from 10 to 1 on each out breath as you walk along the path or down the steps.

- When you get to the bottom of the path or steps imagine yourself in your favourite place of relaxation.

- In your favourite place make it as real as possible, notice the colours, sounds, smells, etc. Really enjoy your favourite place.

- Whilst in your favourite place give yourself positive suggestions about what's going on in your life or what you want to achieve. See it in your mind. Here are just a few suggestions:

  'I am calm and relaxed and feel great about myself.'

  'I am always satisfied with a small meal; I eat healthy nutritious foods.'

  'I dance well, with ease and grace.'

  'As soon as my head touches the pillow, I drift off into a deep and restful sleep.'

- When you are finished begin to count yourself up from 1 to 10.

- While counting up from 1 to 10 tell yourself how wonderful and optimistic you are going to feel as you wake up on the count of 10 and open your eyes.

Self hypnosis is an incredible tool and one we each have at our disposal 24 hours a day. The benefits can be magical if only we take the time and effort to get to know ourselves and sit quietly for a few moments each day. The beautiful thing about self hypnosis is that once you have reached that relaxed state, you can create a whole new world of possibilities and opportunities by telling yourself positive things and visualising what you want as having already happened. The only golden rule is to always tell yourself things in the positive. I know people who have tried self hypnosis and have given up after the first session with themselves for one of two reasons:

1. They couldn't stop the mind chatter – their mind kept wandering.

2. They couldn't get a clear enough image in their mind.

Remember, repetition is the mother of skill. Both of these issues are fixed with practice. Don't give up, the dividends are phenomenal.

> *"The conscious mind may be compared to a fountain playing in the sun and falling back into the great subterranean pool of subconscious from which it rises."*
>
> *Sigmund Freud*

Chapter 11

Stop searching outside of yourself

"You are, at this moment, standing, right in the middle of your own 'acres of diamonds.'"

Earl Nightingale

I remember listening to Earl Nightingale tell a very old story of an African farmer who having toiled for many years on his farm became aware of news spreading across Africa of diamonds being found across the land and of many of his fellow countrymen becoming extremely rich through finding them. Tired of toiling with little to show for years of hard work he decided that he too would find his fortune and quickly sold his farm and travelled the continent in search of riches. After several years the farmer became very despondent and depressed, as despite his exhaustive travels and searching he had not found a single diamond. In complete despair he threw himself into the river and killed himself. Meanwhile, back at the farm he had sold on, the new owner was one day crossing a small stream on the land he had bought when he noticed a blue and white shiny light bouncing off a stone in the stream. He picked the stone up admiring its shape and colour, took it home and placed it as an ornament in his home.

Several weeks later a friend visiting the farm noticed the stone and looking quite stunned asked the farmer where he had acquired it. The farmer explained it was just one of many in his stream but that it was one of the largest. His friend somewhat knowledgeable about gems explained that the stone was no ordinary stone but was in fact a diamond. Not any diamond but it was one of the largest diamonds to be found in Africa. It didn't take long for the new farmer to gather up these diamonds to become one of the wealthiest men in Africa.

The original farmer went off in search of riches when all the time they lay within his grasp. Wealth beyond his wildest imagination lay just yards from where he slept at night, yet he had no idea and instead went off and searched for years for that which had already belonged to him.

I believe this story serves as a metaphor for many of us searching for riches. We may not be looking for diamonds or money or wealth, we could be looking for purpose or love or happiness. Whatever we may be searching for the story suggests it is already within us. Within each of us lies our very own acres of diamonds, resources so great and so powerful that we need never look any further than ourselves. I believe that the greatest diamond of all is our mind and within our mind we know of at least six other priceless diamonds: perception, will, imagination, memory, intuition and reason. I have only chosen to refer to these six diamonds but the human mind and spirit are fraught with infinite diamonds of every shape and size and we are only just beginning to find some of them.

A few years ago I achieved a very significant goal in my life working for a major global brand. It really was a lifetime ambition to sit on the board of an organisation with an excellent household name and I achieved it. However, about a year into working for the organisation I found myself extremely unhappy, largely because I had a terrible working relationship with my boss and as a result I didn't look forward to going to work each day. It got so bad I made a decision to leave and started to look around in the newspapers and on the internet for another job. The job I was unhappy with was based 170 miles away from home, so I found myself travelling away on a Sunday night, staying away all week and returning to my family on a Friday evening after work. Shortly after beginning my search for a new job I found myself at Kings Cross station in London one Sunday evening, because I had decided to change my routine and travel up by train rather than drive, which I normally did. I have no idea why I decided to do that, I guess I just fancied a change and was tired of driving.

Sometimes you just need to get the message

Well, something strange happened that night. I arrived at King's Cross to find my train slightly delayed so I took the opportunity to have a look around a book shop at the station and thought I would buy a book to read on the train as the journey would be just over 1 hour long. I found myself attracted to a book called *The Alchemist* by Paulo Coelho and I settled down to read it. Now I wouldn't normally be able to read over two hundred pages in just a little over an hour. I found myself really engrossed in this book not wanting the train journey to end until I had finished it and then suddenly a half an hour from reaching my destination the train stopped and remained stationary in the middle of nowhere for about another hour, something to do with a problem with the tracks further down the line.

Under normal circumstances I would have been pretty disturbed and frustrated by having my journey delayed by an hour, especially late on a Sunday night. However, this time it was different; I became completely oblivious to the time or delay and continued reading this brilliant little book. As soon as I had read the last page the train moved again.

The reason I am telling you this story is because the book contained a message for me that night and something mystical happened to ensure I received the message. Why did I decide to get the train when I normally drove? Why was the train delayed? Why did I decide to buy a book? Why that book? Why did the train get stuck for an hour?

Well, I won't tell you what the book was about because I don't wish to spoil it for you as it is definitely worth reading. However, suffice to say it was not hugely dissimilar from *Acres of Diamonds* which I had read many years before and forgotten about. The message *The Alchemist* had for me was to stop searching outside of myself and make the very best of what I had and I would find my fortune. I went to work on the Monday morning with a completely different attitude towards myself, my job, my boss and everything around and within me, and two short years later I achieved a financial reward beyond what I could have hoped for. Now had I not read that book that night on that train I would have left the company within a few weeks or months and missed out on a golden opportunity.

To get off the wheel and become truly fulfilled you must become conscious of your own acres of diamonds and not go searching outside yourself. Go within and polish them one by one until you gleam so bright the light exposes all of the diamonds you have at your disposal. Stopping your wheel doesn't mean quitting your job; it does mean understanding who you are, what you are capable of and what you want. It's about recognising your own acres of diamonds and the infinite possibilities they allow you. In its simplest form, if your job is an issue as it was for me, it may just be about viewing it and you in a whole new way. Remember 'when you change the way you look at things, the things you look at change.'

Sometimes the grass isn't always greener on the other side; sometimes you just need a different perspective. You can't get that perspective whilst running furiously on that wheel. It helps enormously if you know what it is that you want.

What do you really want?

When you can answer that question then you can build a true vision for your life and use all of your gifts and diamonds to work towards it, but first, you must be clear on what exactly it is that you want.

When you are running furiously on the treadmill the last thing you have time for is vision; it's more about surviving than thriving into the future. But now you are off your wheel and are wide awake there is no excuse. It's imperative that you have a clear and exciting vision for the future, one that makes you want to jump out of bed in the morning because you cant wait to get started and one that leaves you so energised that you don't even want to really stop at night.

Successful people always have a clear, compelling vision for the future; they look ahead to the future and invest all of their time, effort and energy in making it real. Project yourself forward in your mind 3–5 years and imagine your ideal future vision. What does it look like? What steps can you take immediately to begin turning your future vision into your current reality? Once you are clear then decide in advance that, no matter what happens, you will stay focused, cool, calm and collected and always focus on the vision and solutions to achieving it, rather than dwelling on the problems and obstacles which overwhelm so many.

What exactly is your vision for your life, for your family, for your health and for your career? If you go on any journey, then you have to have some real idea of where it is you want to end up. Can you imagine getting in your car not having a clue as to where it is you want to go? Well, it goes without saying that life is the biggest and most important journey you will ever embark upon, so it makes good sense to have a clear idea of where you want to end up. Don't rely on luck or chance or hope like so many do; be bold and true to yourself and write down where you want to get to in life. The fact is that if you have a clear vision, then the very fact that you have been able to conceive it means you have the power to make it happen, providing of course you have already agreed with yourself that you are willing to do whatever it takes. A vision is a picture you have in your mind of where you want to be; it's a fact that the clearer the picture in your mind then the less fear, the less doubt and the less confusion there is. It's normally these three devils that stop people from achieving their dreams.

Most people assume that to have a vision they have to have a 20-year plan and it has to be SMART. That's all well and good if you know precisely what it is that you want, but if you don't, it can stop most of us from even seriously thinking about it let alone writing it down. I'm here to tell you that you must not let detail get in your way; don't create a huge obstacle before you even start by worrying about detail if you don't have it. A true vision doesn't have to be specific and it doesn't have to be tied to any real time frame or deadline. I often find it's far more powerful to first of all create the big picture and write that down. You might even say what I said, 'I want to connect with as many people as I can to increase their levels of awareness and help them to lead the best lives possible.'

Whatever your vision is write it down, read it and focus on it every day. Most people who bother to have a vision at all tend to just focus on work, and as you have already seen to lead a truly fulfilled life you need to focus and create a vision for every area of your life that is important to you. For my health I wrote, 'I want to have a healthy and flexible body, building muscle, strength, stamina and endurance to give me the energy I need to be successful and happy and to keep my immune system strong and healthy and to keep me young and fit.'

For my family I wrote, 'I want to be the best husband, father, son and brother that I can be, always caring for my family and doing the best that I can to love, help and support them, being a joy to live with.'

One of the certainties of life is that we are all going to come across problems, obstacles and challenges and some of them will be pretty major. However, if we can be clear and true to our vision and focus on it with purpose and clarity we will always be able to overcome those three little devils of fear, doubt and confusion. The clearer the image the more likely we are to succeed. Here are some things to think about when you are thinking about your vision for your life:

- What do you enjoy doing more than anything else in the world?

- What must you do every single day to feel fulfilled in your work?

- What are your five most important values?

- Consider your rollercoaster of reality and write a vision for each important area of your life.

- If you never had to work another day in your life, how would you spend your time instead of working?

- When your life is ending, what will you regret not doing, seeing, or achieving?

Only you know the answers to all of these questions and you also have within you everything you will ever need to achieve all of the answers. So whatever you do, don't make the mistake that so many make in searching outside yourself.

If it's happiness you want, that's inside too!

Whilst we are on the subject of vision, ask anyone what they want more than anything and most people will tell you they just want to be happy. The sad fact about such an answer is it means the people who say that probably aren't that happy. To make matters worse if you ask them what it will take to make them happy they would probably reel off a list of material things, like a new home or car or even a new or better relationship. I think that's great and I too want the car, home and relationship, but I have learned that these actual physical tangible things don't really make you happy once you've got them. We seem to almost be programmed to chase something under the guise of happiness and as soon as we get it we immediately set a new target for happiness. Now that is all well and good and it's something I would condone under the heading of goal setting and helping us to grow. What I would suggest, however, is rather than postponing happiness until you achieve something just make the decision every moment of every day to be happy.

Smile a lot, laugh a lot and choose to think only happy thoughts. Each time you find yourself entertaining a negative or destructive thought, shout the word STOP in your mind and see a great big red STOP light and then focus on something that makes you happy. Go back to a happy memory or think about a time when you just felt so good.

You see, happiness is a state of mind; it's a choice and you have an obligation to yourself and your fellow human beings to be happy. Imagine the impact you would have on your relationships at home or work if you chose to be happy in every moment. Imagine the impact on strangers!

Just like energy and enthusiasm, happiness is a highly infectious emotional state. Have you ever tried to be depressed around an openly happy person? It's not impossible but it really is extremely hard. Remember the Law of Dominant Effect we talked about earlier whereby a stronger emotion will always inhibit a weaker one? Well, that applies to happiness; if you think happy thoughts, surround yourself with happy people, smile, read happy books and watch only happy TV programmes and only say happy things, guess what you will always feel – that's right, happy!

Here are some tips on how to be happy:

- Do something you love – If you hate your job, do everything you can to find something you love about it and to change the way you feel about it. If you still hate it then change your job. Do something you love.

- Be yourself – Don't let people get you down because you are trying to live up to their expectations. Fall in love with who you are and just be you. Never compare yourself with others; focus on being you and let other people see the real you. Remember deep within you are acres of diamonds so don't go searching outside of yourself.

- Get and stay healthy – The most common reason for people dragging themselves down and not being happy is because they don't take responsibility for themselves and look after themselves. Don't make that mistake; get and stay healthy.

- Practise giving – One of the best ways I know to feel happy is to give of myself, my time, energy, kindness, money, effort. Give to other people less fortunate than you and don't look for a return; just do it and you will feel happy.

- Relax – Make sure you schedule quality time to do nothing except be yourself and relax. Get still, stay quiet and calm and just be you for a few moments each day. Breathe deep and enjoy the time to yourself.

- Decide your purpose and set yourself inspirational goals against that purpose. Understand why it is you do what you choose to do and do it with zest and passion.

- Treat everyone you come into contact with including yourself as if they were the most important person on this earth and mean it.

- Develop strong relationships with your family and make sure you find the right partner. You only get the one family and whatever happens deep down you love them and they love you. Don't wait until it's too late to show it.

- Have fun and choose your friends carefully.

- If you remember nothing else remember this – YOU BECOME WHAT YOU THINK ABOUT SO CHOOSE YOUR THOUGHTS CAREFULLY.

"There are lots of ways of being miserable, but there's only one way of being comfortable, and that is to stop running round after happiness."

Edith Wharton

Chapter 12

Remember what you are

"Nobody realizes that some people expend tremendous energy merely to be normal."

Albert Camus

On my journey and quest for knowledge as to exactly what it is that makes some people successful and lead extraordinary lives whilst others 'tiptoe through life hoping to make it safely to death', I couldn't help asking myself the question 'what are we?' and is there some universal force or power that is greater than us? Two very deep questions, I know, and one could argue that the answers are considerably deeper. It was one of my mentors Bob Proctor who suggested to me that if you want answers there are really only two places you can go: you can look to science or look to theology. He went on to explain that if you ask a scientist what we are made of and whether there is a power or force in the universe greater than us he or she will say words to the effect: There is a power in the universe which is both ubiquitous and all pervasive, it exists in all places at all times and cannot be created or destroyed, it just is. We call it energy. If you then go to a theologian and ask him or her exactly the same question you will hear the answer: There is a power in the universe which is both ubiquitous and all pervasive, it exists in all places at all times and cannot be created or destroyed, it just is. We call it God.

Now I am neither a scientist nor a theologian so it's really difficult to get to the bottom of this one, although what I do know is that their answers are remarkably similar with the exception of what we call this power. Scientifically it has been proven that everything in the universe is energy including us. Behind the atoms and molecules of every living and non-living thing is energy. The only reason everything appears so different is the frequency at which that energy is vibrating.

The fact I find really interesting is, that whether you choose to believe in the concept of god or not, you can't not believe in the scientific realisation of energy, because it's real. If you accept this fact and accept that as human beings our entire existence is a construct of energy, can you believe that many of us are wandering around the planet complaining to each other that 'we have no energy'. Going as far back as the 1950s, DuPont scientists said that every human being has 11 million kilowatt hours of energy per pound of the body, enough to light up their entire town for a whole week. Yet we still say we have no energy.

We have all the energy we need yet we make conscious and unconscious choices every single day to quell that energy by the toxic way we live our lives. Think about the natural energy you have and how you perform a daily ritual of stifling and destroying that energy through the consumption of so many toxins, cigarettes, alcohol, drugs (prescribed and non-prescribed), fattening sweets, sickly unhealthy foods, too much salt, too much sugar, and lack of exercise. Of course it's not just what we choose to put into our bodies physically that reduces this natural energy, it's also what we choose to put into our minds mentally and emotionally that's just as much an issue, if not in many cases a far greater problem.

Remember we established quite a while back that it's our thoughts that drive our emotions that drive our behaviours that cause our results. So if we are thinking toxic thoughts it then follows that we will have toxic feelings which will cause us to behave badly and get results we really don't want.

Think back to a time when you were angry, sad or depressed and recall how this made you feel and the results of those feelings and behaviours. Maybe you went straight to the pub or for the chocolate cake or just locked yourself up for days draining your own energy.

We are pure energy!

The point I am trying to make is that we are energy. We are energy but at times we may feel as though we have no energy and the reason for that is nothing more than our lifestyle: a combination of what we put into our minds and bodies. The good news as you already know from the essence of this entire book is that we have the power to change it, both quickly and permanently, and have all the energy we want by changing our lifestyles and our thoughts.

Here we go, I know, 'that's easier said than done'. You promised us both you wouldn't say that, of course it's easier said than done. The fact is though if you really, really want more energy you will make that choice, make that decision and change. Why would you settle for anything less? You already know from hard practical experience that the times you felt at your very best in life were when you had high energy; you know that you need high energy to achieve your goals and dreams and that you need high energy to just be happy. So make a commitment to stop telling yourself how little energy you have and to change it, change your thoughts, change your feelings, change your behaviours, and change your life. High energy is your natural birthright. It's already a part of you; all you have to do is to reclaim it.

Here are 10 tips for increasing your energy levels:

1. Watch what you eat and drink. Focus on eating healthy well-balanced meals. Don't diet, just eat nutritious food. Drink plenty of water because there is nothing worse than dehydration, which can exhaust your body of its store of energy. Lose the weight if you are carrying too much, as this can contribute to tiredness. Nutritional supplements can be a good thing dependent upon the types of foods you eat – get advice from a nutritionist.

2. Expose yourself to natural light, get yourself out in daylight. A severe lack of natural light can cause so many different problems, ranging from irritability, fatigue and insomnia, right through to depression. Spend as much time as you can outside. Walk to your local park, the shops or work and get out in nature as often as you can. Open the curtains and let in the sunshine.

3. Make sure you get enough sleep, the amount of sleep that you need. If in doubt experiment until you find the right level for you. Whatever you do never compromise your energy levels by not getting enough sleep.

4. Exercise at least three times a week. Make sure you focus on your breathing too as most people simply do not breathe properly. Try breathing deeply instead of shallowly taking deep breaths through your nose and then exhaling through your mouth.

5. Stop worrying. Worrying is a complete waste of time and the greatest energy thief, it has never helped anyone. Forty per cent of your worries will never ever happen, 30 per cent of the things you worry about are in the past and have already happened, 12 per cent of your worries are unnecessary worries about health, 10 per cent of worries are other peoples and only 8 per cent are real, so stop worrying. Of the 8 per cent that are real, half of them you can do something about and the other half you can't, so for the ones you have control over think about solutions instead of worrying thoughts. For the remainder you have no control over, worrying is never going to help, so use your energy to prepare for the outcome.

6. Surround yourself only with people who inspire you and make you feel good. Your friends will either lift you up or drag you down, so choose them wisely. Avoid energy thieves like the plague.

7. Choose your attitude and response to everything. Stay positive.

8. Listen to lively music.

9. Act energetic, keep moving and get things done.

10. There are a number of medical conditions which can cause tiredness. Get your doctor to check you over if you remain concerned.

Whatever you think you are, you are here to have fun too!

I don't know about you but I love to have fun and I tend to associate fun with having a good laugh and just feeling totally free and at ease. Having fun can dramatically increase your energy levels and sense of happiness. Even though I am all grown up I still like playing. I also know that when I get so wrapped up in life and work I sometimes forget to have fun and I pay the price. Laughter alone activates chemicals and hormones which have an amazingly positive effect on our body and mind. A genuine and real hearty laugh can help to:

- reduce stress,

- lower blood pressure,

- elevate mood,

- boost immune system,

- improve brain functioning,

- protect the heart,

- connect you to others,

- increase relaxation,

- make you feel good.

Have you noticed how some of the most successful people in the world, and I define success as a balanced lifestyle (health, wealth, peace, harmony and happiness), have the most fun. They know how to work hard and play hard and laugh out loud.

Do whatever it takes to have fun, whatever it is that makes you feel alive, that makes you smile, makes you laugh and feel good inside. Don't take yourself or others too seriously. Schedule time on your to do list if you absolutely have to, but make sure you have fun. Try to see the lighter and funnier side of everything; try to bring humour to every area of your life that you can and every interaction with others, even strangers. Make people laugh and make yourself laugh. Read funny books, go to see funny films or shows, watch the reruns of your favourite childhood comedy shows, and let yourself go from time to time. Step outside the box of your own entertainment and do something different, something you wouldn't normally do or haven't tried before. Sometimes stepping outside of your comfort zone can be fun too if you just let it.

Define what fun means to you, as you can stop 100 people in the street and ask them what fun means to them and they will all give you different answers, so be clear on what your idea of fun is. I like to think of fun as my way of 'playing', that's right adults still get to play, so how do you like to play? Don't take life so seriously all of the time. Ask yourself where in your life are you too serious, ask your family, your children and your colleagues, then ask them and yourself, what you can and will do to lighten up and have more fun. Let your hair down sometimes, go crazy, make silly faces, play a prank on someone, dress crazy, get someone to tickle your feet if you have to just make sure you set a goal to have fun.

Don't forget to be grateful for what you are and who you are!

One of the strongest emotions in the world is gratitude – being truly grateful, content and happy with what you are, who you are and all that you are and have achieved. The emotion of gratitude is an incredible gift that most of us have either taken for granted, or have no idea exists in a manner in which we both should and could experience it. It is impossible to feel anxious, stressed or angry whilst you are in the middle of feeling truly grateful. Try it some day. No, don't wait for some day, try it now. Eyes open or closed, it doesn't really matter but regardless of how little you may have in your life, or all of the problems or nasty things which may have happened to you in the past, think of only the good things no matter how small.

People who express gratitude report much higher levels of satisfaction in their lives, feel more optimistic and enjoy far greater amounts of energy. Increasing research suggests that people who regularly and sincerely express feelings of gratitude can also improve their overall physical health and functioning. Gratitude can go as far as to manifest itself in positive changes in an individual's cardiovascular and immune functioning.

Studies have demonstrated that people who focused on being grateful rather than on not being angry were found to positively impact a variety of important physiological functions such as improved heart, pulse, and respiration rates. There is no doubt now that gratitude can significantly reduce stress levels. Being grateful is much more than just saying thank you. Real gratitude is felt from the heart and experienced and felt frequently. To be grateful is to appreciate even the smallest things in your life which most of us take for granted.

It starts with being grateful for just being alive and being who you are, warts and all. Being grateful for being able to breathe the air you breathe and being able to see the sun rise and set. It's being grateful for your home, your health, your family and relationships, for everything you own and have ever owned, for every one of your experiences good and bad which have helped you to learn and grow, for your education and the ability to laugh and cry, to think and dance and listen to music, to be able to speak, touch, and smell and hear, to be able to feel and know what you are feeling, and to be able to change your feelings in an instant.

Have you ever stopped to think about the fact that there are billions of people existing on this planet who would give everything to experience the freedom that you feel to live your life the way you choose? Have you thought of the countless number of people who in so many different ways are far worse off than you, yet still find the time to smile and be grateful? When you go to bed at night tucked up so snugly in the duvet, give a thought to the homeless, and when you dine out in McDonalds or your favourite Michelin star restaurant think about the millions starving around the world. When you go home from a hard day's work sulking because your boss gave you a hard time, or you didn't get the pay rise you deserve think about the millions of people who would trade places with you in a heartbeat.

Gratitude requires self reflection and full acknowledgement and use of your six intellectual gifts. There is much to be grateful for whoever you are and wherever you are and whatever your circumstances. Go for a walk every so often for 30 minutes or so and think about everything in your life that you have to be grateful for and really feel it.

Make it a habit

Since watching a brilliant film on the Law of Attraction called *The Secret* I have created for myself a habit of feeling grateful each morning as I rise and each night as I go to bed. I do this by using a very simple process shown on *The Secret* of carrying what I call a gratitude stone around with me all day in my trouser pocket. It's always there, so when I go to bed at night and empty my trouser pockets I find my gratitude stone, place it on the dressing table and I spend a few minutes going to bed thinking about so many of the things I have been blessed with in my life. When I wake up in the morning and go to get dressed I pick my gratitude stone up off the dressing table and think about all of the wonderful things in my life no matter how small.

When I'm stuck in traffic, rather than get hot and bothered, angry and frustrated, I reach into my pocket and pull out my gratitude stone and become grateful for the time to myself to just think and be grateful and imagine all the things I have to become grateful for. When I'm stuck in a long queue in a supermarket and it looks like I'm going to be there forever, I reach for my stone and feel grateful for the luxury of being able to shop and all the times I have been able to do so and the freedom in which I can do it. I chose my gratitude stone from my father's grave when I went to visit him on his birthday. It was an ordinary stone, but one that caught my eye as I gazed around the cemetery looking at all of those people who expended so much of their time on earth worrying and complaining and never being happy with what they had. As I looked around me I thought of the death of all of those dreams not the death of the bodies, and as I looked at the stone it started me thinking about how grateful I was to have known my father and to still be here to dare and to dream. Now it goes everywhere with me.

Whenever I have a problem, am feeling stuck, lonely or sorry for myself I pull out my gratitude stone and focus on all that I have had and still have instead of all that's missing. Try it for yourself, it really helps. You don't have to have a stone, maybe you may choose to use a rubber band, a small piece of crystal or an acorn, anything will do.

Know what you stand for as well as what you are!

I really believe that we should all make the time and effort to understand what we are and that when we have a reasonable grasp about that, we should then begin to think about what we stand for.

When I worked for that insurance company many years ago and I was asked by the executive to relocate to do my best to turn the performance of another much larger business unit around, one of the ideas I came up with was introducing a mascot. At the time the business was performing so badly it really was only months away from closure for being too costly. Whilst thinking about what I could do to help save it, I remembered a story I had read a few years previously about a travel agent in the USA who had opened up a brand new business and his vision was to be bigger and better than his competition. He decided at the outset that whatever the competition did, he would do things differently but much better.

One day very early on into the operation he sat down with his team and suggested that for a bit of fun maybe it would be a good idea if they introduced a mascot into the business, something that would reflect the values of the business and what they believed they stood for and how they would behave. Everyone thought it was a great idea and the owner asked for suggestions as to what they thought the mascot should be. Immediately someone came up with the idea of a salmon. They explained that as the owner continuously asked them to behave differently and to always seek an opposite but better path to the competition, it had to be a salmon because a salmon always swims upstream, against the tide or the general flow of everything else. Instantly they all agreed and adopted the salmon as their mascot and over the years they had enormous fun and considerable success relating to the salmon.

With this in mind I took this idea to this failing business and suggested maybe it would help us if we had a mascot, something we could all relate to that would remind us of our values, what we stood for and where we were heading. After much discussion and persuasion the team finally agreed (although I have no doubt that they believed that both I and my suggestion were crazy).

Like the travel agent, I had no idea what our mascot should be so I asked the team to come up with an idea that would work for everyone. Well, ideas started flowing in and some good ones at that, so the only way to decide was to turn it into a competition and let the business vote. Well, we ended up with hundreds of ideas, but to cut a long story short, the idea with an overwhelming amount of votes was a dragon.... that's right a dragon. Now this was back in 1997 and we were building a vision for the year 2000, and so one creative soul suggested that as the year 2000 was the Year of the Dragon under the Chinese horoscope it should be the dragon. Now given that no one in the business was Chinese and no one had much knowledge of these things, it seemed more than a little strange at the time until of course he revealed his logic.

The suggestion was made because under this sign the characteristics of the dragon were: energetic, decisive, dynamic, bold, etc... so the person who suggested the dragon was adamant that if we were going to succeed with our vision and turn the business around, these were the attributes we all needed to convey.

This received unanimous support, so our mascot became a dragon. We didn't stop there though, we had another competition to give it a name and the winning name was:

Dynamic

Understanding

Decisive

Leading

Energetic

Youthful

We didn't stop there either, someone suggested we gave it a real image and identity, so away we went with another competition and drawings and cartoon dragons came flying in from every corner of the business until finally DUDLEY came alive.

Now the reason for telling you all of this is because DUDLEY gave that whole business a new lease of life, it gave it a set of clear values to live and work by, and within a year we turned the entire business around thanks to our new mascot DUDLEY. Now you may still ask what on earth this has to do with you. Well, I believe that we all need to be clear on what it is we stand for; we need to identify, understand and be crystal clear on our values and then live by them every single day. I still live by DUDLEY in my personal life today and maybe, just maybe, it would help you to consider creating your very own personal mascot. Of course if this is too much trouble for you then that's fine too, but don't overlook the importance of being absolutely clear on what it is you stand for, writing it down and reminding yourself everyday.

Here are some other examples of values: **ambition, competency, individuality, equality, integrity, service, responsibility, accuracy, respect, dedication, diversity, improvement, enjoyment/fun, loyalty, credibility, honesty, innovativeness, teamwork, excellence, accountability, empowerment, quality, efficiency, dignity, collaboration, stewardship, empathy, accomplishment, courage, wisdom, independence, security, challenge, influence, learning, compassion, friendliness, discipline, generosity, persistence, optimism, dependability, flexibility**

Choose the values that are most important to you, the values you believe in and that define who you are and who you choose to be – your character. Then live them visibly every day at work and at home. Living your values is one of the most powerful things you can do to help you be the person you want to be, to help you accomplish your goals and dreams, and to help you lead and influence others.

*"Try not to become a man of success
but a man of value."*

Albert Einstein

Chapter 13

Make it happen

"God is really only another artist, he made the elephant, giraffe and cat. He has no real style but keeps trying new ideas"

Pablo Picasso

'Heavier than air flying machines are impossible.' These were the words of Lord Kelvin of the Royal Society in 1895 and he wasn't alone; many, many others said it would be impossible to build a machine to fly in the sky. Aren't you glad the Wright brothers proved them all wrong? I know I certainly am.

'Who the hell wants to hear actors talk?' These were the words of H.M. Warner of Warner Brothers films back in 1927. Well, aren't you glad that Warner Brothers changed their mind? I know I am, because going to the cinema is one of my favourite activities and I couldn't imagine going to see a film where the actors didn't talk.

'We don't like their sound, and guitar music is on the way out.' These were the words of the Decca Recording Company in 1962 making reference to a band you may have heard of called The Beatles.

'This "telephone" has too many shortcomings to be seriously considered as a means of communication. The device is inherently of no value to us.' This was a statement made by a US telegraph company Western Union in 1876. Do you find the telephone useful?

'There is no reason for any individual to have a computer in their home.' These are the famous words of Kenneth Olsen, president and founder of Digital Equipment Corp in 1977. Do you have a computer in your home?

'Space travel is utter bilge.' – Dr Richard van der Reit Wooley, Astronomer Royal, space advisor to the British government, 1956.

'The horse is here to stay, but the automobile is only a novelty – a fad.' This was advice from a president of the Michigan Savings Bank to Henry Ford's lawyer Horace Rackham. Rackham ignored the advice and invested $5000 in Ford stock, selling it later for $12.5 million. GET THE PICTURE!

We've already talked about how much the world has changed and continues to change at an incredible pace, and the simple fact is these changes occur as a result of just two things: people and ideas. Ideas emanate from thought and most of us spend much of our time hoping for good ideas yet that's all we tend to do, just hope and wish that ideas come to us as if they arrive by magic. It's been my experience that many people think that ideas only flow to those people who are either lucky or highly intellectual, and neither is true. You see, everything that exists and surrounds you in the world you live in today always existed. All of the things you see around you no matter how big or small, simple or complex, only came into physical reality through awareness.

What I mean by that is that absolutely everything created by man only became a physical reality by someone, somewhere, creating a genuine desire for something and expanding their entire awareness about the desire. It's been my experience that the process for the generation of ideas is really no different from the process for achieving or experiencing anything you want in your life. The brilliant news is that every person on this planet has all of the intellectual gifts to generate any idea they want, all they have to do is to practise using their gifts and get good at using them. Don't rely on luck, or hope or magic. Use your gift of thought to create whatever it is you want. Never sit around waiting for things to happen!

The reality is, this changing world thrives on creative thinking, it is driven by ideas and no one on the planet has the monopoly on this creative power and our ability to generate ideas. So when you look at your rollercoaster of reality and you consider the many different areas of your life, set goals for each area you need to and then you can very easily generate all of the ideas you need for the most positive and fulfilling goals imaginable for you. To create ideas you have to expend time, energy and thought. You have to commit to an objective of generating the ideas. Don't just wait for them to pop up randomly whilst you are in the shower or on the toilet. This will happen sometimes, but make it easier on yourself by increasing your entire awareness on how to generate ideas so that they more readily and frequently come to you whilst in the shower or on the toilet. Try this:

- **Be precise** – You massively increase your chance of success if you are crystal clear on your goal or objective. If it's a problem you are trying to solve then write down in very specific terms exactly what the problem is and everything it affects. If it's an opportunity or something you want then again write it down and be very specific in terms of the outcome you are looking for.

- **Create a stimulating environment** – When sitting down to think, listen to a piece of unusual or different music. Take a walk in nature, go and sit in a cathedral or museum, take yourself somewhere different to think. Play Christmas carols in the middle of summer or buy a birthday cake and light candles when it isn't your birthday.

- **Use post it notes** – Play a little game with yourself and write down as many ideas as you can on post it notes and see how much of the wall you can cover with them.

- **Mind storm and brain storm** – Firstly, sit quietly on your own with a pen and notepad and write down everything you can possibly think of which could be a solution or opportunity for the problem or goal. Just let it flow, write whatever comes into your mind as crazy, silly or even as impossible as it may seem at the time, write as much as you can as fast as you can. When you think you have exhausted yourself push for another three ideas. Also, find a group of people to brainstorm with. A brainstorm is exactly the same as a mind storm, but using the collective minds and imaginations of a group of people who would like to help you succeed or share the same objective. Don't stop to discuss or analyse any of the ideas, just encourage crazy creativity and let it flow. Focus on quantity not quality!

- **Focus just on you** – Think only about what you truly want and why you want it. Forget everything and everyone else for now. Think about how achieving your goal will make you feel and all of the good that will come from it and what it will do for you.

- **Check your passion** – Sometimes we get involved in things or ideas that we aren't too interested in. Always check your passion for what you are looking at and working on. Make sure it's definitely something that turns you on. If it isn't you will struggle to get those creative juices flowing.

- **Expose yourself to new experiences** – Go out of your way to experience different situations, people, places, foods, books, magazines, shows and events as the more you broaden your mind the more the ideas will flow. Really welcome variety in your life and never be afraid of doing things differently.

- **Look at each task as a challenge** – Never think of a problem as a problem, always see it as a challenge or opportunity. The very word problem has negative connotations and therefore stifles creativity.

- **Let your creative subconscious work for you** – Let your subconscious mind go to work for you. Put yourself into a state of self hypnosis, present the opportunity or challenge to your subconscious mind and just wait and see what happens. Your subconscious is always working for you.

- **Carry a notepad** – Make a point of capturing all of your ideas. Don't take the risk of forgetting them, carry a notepad and pencil with you everywhere.

- **Be grateful for ideas** – Encourage your mind to come up with more new ideas by always being grateful and thankful for the ones you do have.

- **Think of the greater good** – Try to think how what you are doing will help not just you but others too. When you are looking for something for the greater good of others you are more likely to find it.

While you are busy achieving, don't forget to enjoy the journey!

It's great to have goals; in fact in my view it's essential. It's the very act of having a goal that serves to direct, inspire, challenge, motivate and stretch us, helping us to grow and enjoy life more fully, and become all that we possibly can during our short spell on this planet. It is, however, always worth remembering that our time on this planet is brief and if we adopt the attitude of simply setting and achieving goal, after goal, after goal with complete disregard for the journey, the goals ultimately become pointless.

Have you ever noticed how the moment you achieve a goal you immediately start thinking about the next one? That's all well and good as goal setting is a creative process whereby once you have achieved your objective you should build a bigger and better fantasy and move onto that and continue the cycle. However, you should never lose sight of the fact that the real growth and the real excitement comes whilst you are on the journey. Sure the momentary euphoria comes at the end when you can finally say 'I did it' but there are many, many more moments before you get to that point. These are the moments which should be acknowledged, appreciated and enjoyed.

Have you ever organised a surprise birthday party, or planned a special holiday or a trip to the theatre with someone you care about? Well, you may very well recall that sometimes you found the actual organising, planning and arranging of the event more enjoyable than the end result, the goal itself. My point is, it is as much, if not more, about the journey than the destination itself. Sometimes we achieve something great or special and at the end we stand back and ask ourselves how on earth we achieved it. Sometimes we are so blinkered and focused on the outcome that we go on autopilot and shut off our senses and some of our intellectual faculties on the journey.

There was a time when I was much younger when I would save all year long to go on holiday. So I'd set the goal of basking in the sun for two whole weeks and when the time finally arrived I found myself lying on the beach thinking about all the things I had to do back at work. There was a time when I didn't really enjoy the journey, where all I was focused on was the clock, getting things done, achieving the goal and moving on. I learned to change and the way I did that was by reflecting on each day. At the end of each day, a good hour or so before I knew I was going to bed, I locked myself away for a quiet 10 minutes and replayed my day. I thought about all the things I did and how they made me feel. At the beginning of each new day as I got myself ready to start the day or go off to work I spent another 10 minutes thinking about how I would make an effort to slow down and become more aware of what was happening to me and how I felt during the day. It changed everything because it made me more conscious and increased my awareness of me and how I was thinking, feeling and behaving each day and therefore the impact I had on the direction I was taking and the results I was achieving (or not).

When you're frustrated, in a rush, trying to juggle your time and responsibilities between work and home, remember why you're doing this...and discover joy in the journey. Look at your accomplishments and activities each day, no matter how small; enjoy and celebrate those along the way. This will make it easier to overcome obstacles and reach your ultimate goal.

Part of making things happen means you have to keep changing!

At the very start of this book I made reference to the world changing so fast and it's true. We have seen more profound change in the last 150 years than we have in the history of the entire world. Largely, the changes are brilliant, they are for the best, but often we tend to focus and dwell on the negatives, the bad things. When people think about change they often associate change with discomfort, loss or pain and that's why you hear so may people especially in the workplace talk about and long for 'the good old days'. The fact is that change isn't just about yesterday or last year or even 20 years ago, change is about now. Change is about today and it's not something we should be scared about. We simply can't change all of the outside events and things that are going to happen to us, but we can change and manage how we feel about any event or circumstance in our lives if we see change for what it really is – growth. You see, I don't believe that anything ever really stands still. Given that we and the entire universe are made of energy and that energy is in a constant state of vibration, we are always moving whether we like it or not.

I look at it this way: from the very second we are born we start to grow and we continue to grow right up to the very second of our death. Most people would associate this growth with just the physical body and call it aging and that's true of course because it's part of the process of life. However, it's not just the body, our mind is also growing too; we are learning and experiencing new things every day of our lives. We are creatures of habit and so much of our lives are lived through habit; we get comfortable with the way things are. As our comfort increases, if anything arises to challenge, disturb or threaten that comfort, we immediately begin to resent and fight it. Whilst that is maybe the way it is for many of us, it isn't the way it should be.

As human beings we need to be absolutely certain that we will always have enough to eat and drink, that we will always have a roof over our heads and the warmth we need and enough money to care for ourselves and our families. Once we have that level of basic certainty we then need a level of uncertainty or variety to make and keep life interesting. The people who are 'tiptoeing through life hoping to make it safely to death' are the people only focused on that certainty and are both afraid of and lack the uncertainty in their lives. Can you imagine a life where every single day is the same, where nothing ever changes, where you have no problems or surprises, where nothing new or different ever happens? Where's the fun in that, where's the life? Surely life wasn't designed to be lived that way. That was the life my old friend Botley lived every day on the wheel.

Yet that's the trap that some of us fall into because we get so comfortable that we become terrified of disrupting the status quo. The fact is change is good; it's healthy because it fulfils two more of our human needs: uncertainty and growth. Change brings variety, challenge, stimulation and growth; it keeps us alive and keeps us on the edge. Even bad change is good change, because it stretches us to find a new way. I tend to find that the people who don't know about, think about or understand their intellectual faculties are the people who tend to fear change the most. The secret to change is to understand these gifts, to develop them and most importantly use them every single day.

You quite often hear the generalisation 'people don't like change', well, I think the truth is 'people don't like being changed'. After all, who in their right mind likes to be forced to do something they may neither like, agree with nor even understand? I know I wouldn't. However, when I myself want change and see the need for it, well, that's a different story altogether. I believe that we should not only welcome change but that we should actively encourage it.

It pays to re-invent yourself

A good way of doing this is to re-invent yourself every few years. Look at everything about your life, who you are, the way you think, the way you dress, speak, act, what you eat, where you live, who your friends are, what books you read, music you listen to, movies you watch, holidays you go on, route you drive to work, etc, etc, etc, and then challenge them and change some of them. It's not about comfort – after all, most of the things you will be doing will be comfortable simply because they have become habit – it's about growth. I believe that's why we are here, to grow, learn, develop and contribute. How do you grow, I mean really grow, if you never step out of your comfort zone and experience change. Do something every day that you have never done before; it may even be as simple as talk to a stranger on the train or make a shopkeeper smile, buy a homeless person some lunch or phone someone you haven't spoken to in years. Do whatever you can to step outside your comfort zone and change. Change is good.

"We must always change, renew, rejuvenate ourselves; otherwise we harden."

Johann Wolfgang von Goethe

Chapter 14

Never give up

"Persistence is the twin sister of excellence. One is a matter of quality; the other, a matter of time."

Marabel Morgan

The hamster never ever gives up, even though he never gets anywhere or achieves anything, he never ever gives up. He will run all day and all night if he has to and if he falls off the wheel he just jumps back on and gets back running.

Now remember two things:

1. The hamster doesn't know what he/she is doing.

2. You are not a hamster, you have the gift of the human brain, the human spirit, the human intellect, the gift of choice and decision, will, imagination, perception, reason, intuition and memory, you have infinite potential and capacity.

Take a brief moment to consider your brain; you have been entrusted with the care and feeding of the most extraordinary and complex creation in the universe. Home to your personality, your brain houses your cherished memories and future hopes and dreams. It allows you the consciousness that gives you purpose and passion, meaning, drive, motion and emotion.

Any eminent scientist, doctor, psychologist, religious or business leader will tell you that you are the caretaker of the most powerful supercomputer which will ever be created at any time, anywhere in the entire universe. With your brain, with your mind and your fathomless ocean of gifts you can do, be or have whatever it is that you want. Now sadly our good friend the hamster doesn't have a tiny fraction of this capacity and potential, yet even the hamster knows never to give up. One of the secrets to fulfilment and harmony is to decide what you really want and to do whatever it takes to get it.

Reasons, reasons, reasons

Before you even begin, you have to be able to answer two very, very important questions. The first question is: 'Are you able to do what it is that you want to do?' Now, if it's physically impossible like you are 5 ft 2 and you really want to be 6 ft 1, then, forget it, that's fantasy. If it's not physically impossible then the answer has to always be 'yes' although that's where so many people fall down and never even get to the second question. They answer NO they are NOT able and 99 times out of 100 it's just not true, it's a blatant lie. It's a story and belief they have created for themselves which they can change, but the reality is only they can finish the story.

Once you have said 'yes, of course I am able' the second important question is: 'Are you willing to do whatever it takes?' And for many people the answer is a quick and resounding NO and the idea, goal or project never even steps out of the imagination. To never give up is making a commitment up front that you are not only able to, but you are willing to do whatever it takes. Here is a list of reasons why most people give up:

- They are not clear what it is they really want, why they want it, what it will do for them and how it will make them feel.

- They don't visualise it and in the absence of a very clear and compelling vision, one you can really see, hear, smell, taste and touch, in their mind it creates fear, doubt and confusion which stops them dead in their tracks.

- They have a story! So whilst they have made a conscious decision to do something they then play the story over and over again about why they would love to and they really tried ...but...

- They are stuck in the habit of their very own comfort zone, keeping things safe, not wanting to rock the boat.

- Fear of failure (see below).

- Time. They think things will happen quickly or even overnight and when it doesn't they say well at least I tried.

- Difficulty. Most people set out full of zest and enthusiasm and then quickly realise that things aren't as easy as they thought they would be so they give up.

- Distractions. Many people get easily distracted as they

set about the project or goal and then quickly forget that life goes on around them as usual and there are other things to be done. It all gets too much.

- Maintenance. The best example I can give of this is dieting. I have always said that diets don't work. Look at the person who really wants to lose weight. Six months pass, they achieve their ideal weight and say great, now I can eat pizza and chocolate cake again. Maintenance is critical.

- Ownership. Many people pick up a self-help book, CD or DVD thinking 'this is the one', 'this will fix me'. The reality is a book won't 'fix you'. Only YOU 'fix you'. The desire, drive and commitment to change has to come from you not a book. The first step to success is personal ownership of YOU.

Fear of failure

This is by far one of the greatest and most debilitating fears people have. Fear of failure is also closely related to fear of criticism and fear of rejection. Fear incapacitates people and to achieve any level of success you have to overcome your fear of failure. I believe that there is no such thing as failure; there is only experience. Successful people look at mistakes as outcomes or results, not as failure. Unsuccessful people look at mistakes as permanent and personal.

When you go back to the time you were a very small child you can appreciate that everything you have learned, absolutely everything has been as a result of trial and error and you have made many, many mistakes along the way, even from the moment you learned to walk. As we grow up and start believing our own stories (most of which were passed down to us from others) many people self-limit themselves. These people do not achieve a fraction of what they are capable of achieving, because they are afraid to try, because they are afraid they will fail.

Here's how to overcome the fear of failure:

- **Change your belief** – instead of telling yourself that if you fail then you are a failure as a human being, tell yourself you would rather not fail but you accept that as a human being you are fallible and you can learn from the experience whatever happens.

- **Take action** – taking action gives you power. Don't hide away or freeze; it just immobilises you and makes it 10 times worse.

- **Picture yourself succeeding** – hold the image in your mind of doing well. Visualise success, make it clear bright and colourful. Feel what it feels like in your mind first.

- **Consider the cost of the lost opportunity** – sometimes it's worth the risk.

- **What's the worst thing that can happen** – ask yourself this and recognise and accept that it's never quite as bad as you imagine.

- **Use self hypnosis** – practise self hypnosis and relaxation to help you overcome your fear.

- **Be clear on your purpose** – make a decision.

- **Remember your physiology, focus and language** – keep an eye on all three.

Part of never giving up means taking risks!

It's a fact that each of us is unconsciously taking risks every day of our lives. If you drive to work, take public transport, walk to work, jump on a train or an aeroplane, or put food in your mouth, you are taking a risk with your life; even when you go to sleep at night you risk not waking up. These are all necessary risks, things we just have to do and if we were to constantly think about them we would create unnecessary anxiety for ourselves.

When most people see someone successful you will often hear them say how lucky that person is, believing that the only real reason they have achieved such fame and fortune is down to luck and being in the right place at the right time.

I believe a small element of luck does often have a role to play; however, I believe there are far more important ingredients involved in success, many of which are contained in this book and all revolve around awareness. You see, you could very easily be in the right place at the right time but if you are not living consciously enough to be aware of that fact you can't take advantage of the opportunity, so it just passes you on by. One critical ingredient of awareness is the ability and confidence to recognise and take risks. No one achieves any real level of success without taking a risk. Imagine what would happen if you were completely risk averse; you would never step outside your front door, you would never explore any new opportunity. Opportunities are everywhere, we live in a world full of opportunities and possibilities; many of us are aware of this fact and so we explore these opportunities in our mind. For many of us though that's as far as it ever goes because we then use our incredible gift of imagination to destroy the opportunity through visualising all the risks. We create a brilliant image of a possibility and then immediately taint the image by seeing all the worst things that could happen.

Once we have finished destroying the idea in our mind we then label it as 'too risky' and the idea is dead. What we need to do is to be aware of the risks and do our due diligence but balance the risk by making the image of success even brighter and more colourful. We then have to do just one thing, the most important thing anyone can do – we have to take action, we have to do something.

Think back to when you were young. As a young child growing up you didn't even understand this thing we call risk. It was completely alien to you. After all, if you wanted to do something you just went ahead and did it; you didn't think about the consequences you just did it. You ate dirt from the garden, ash from the ashtray, you poked your fingers wherever you wanted to and said whatever you wanted to say and didn't give it a second thought. As you grew up you were slowly introduced to the concept of risk by grown ups, and before long you stopped taking risks altogether. You were taught to play it safe. You stayed in your own little 'box' where you felt safe and secure, knowing what you were capable of.

Here is what happened: when you were young, you just did whatever you wanted to do without giving a second thought to the consequences and then as you grew up and got older, you stopped doing the things you really wanted to do because you began thinking about the consequences, of all the things that could go wrong. Two extremes, neither of which is right.

Now, I'm not suggesting that we revert to childhood and forget everything we have been told about risk and consequences, but I am suggesting that we remind ourselves of the fun we had as children without being completely consumed by risk. I am suggesting that we look at risk in a slightly different way whereby we look at the opportunities and possibilities as a journey of exploration.

Asking yourself the right questions keeps you on track!

Life is about communication; we are always communicating in some way, with someone, and the fact is that for the most part that someone is us. When you think about those 60,000 thoughts a day that you have, think about how you think about them and what they do or don't do for you. Think about how those same thoughts every day have brought you to where you are today. You have already looked at your rollercoaster of reality (the different areas of your life) and so by now you have a pretty clear view on exactly what's what in your life.

Interestingly, when most people stand back and look at their life and identify a particular area they are unhappy with, then normally the very first question they ask themselves is 'why?' 'Why does it have to be this way?' 'Why me?' The process of asking why is often a damaging process because all it does is serve to help you find all of the negative reasons and therefore focus on little else but negativity. Whilst then being overwhelmed by the negativity we get 'stuck', unable to think clearly and move on. The best approach is always to ask 'what?' 'What do I need to do to fix this?' 'What do I need to do to take me in the direction of my goal?' 'What can I do to live my dream?'

To live life to the full you need to have a dialogue with yourself. So make an appointment with yourself, sit down in front of the mirror and ask yourself these very important questions:

- What would I do if I could do anything I wanted tomorrow?

- What would I do if I knew I couldn't fail?

- What are my core values; what do I stand for and believe in?

- What do I really, really, really want?

- What do I do better than most people I know?

- What were my dreams as a child?

- What is the thing I am most proud of accomplishing in my life so far?

- What will I regret not doing in my life if I continue as I am now?

- What do I want people to say about me after I'm no longer living?

- What is my legacy?

- What do I want to do when I retire?

- What do I want my life to be about?

- What areas of my life am I short-changing?

- What am I willing to give to achieve my goal?

- What does it mean to be completely fulfilled in my life?

- What do I do that gives me the least joy?

- What do I do that gives me the most joy?

- What's missing in my life?

- What is my purpose?

- What makes me truly happy?

- What three actions could I take right now that would have the biggest positive impact on my life?

Don't just read the questions and not give them any thought and then quickly move on. Answer each question with brutal honesty, reflect on them, be as truthful as you can and read your answers every day for 30 days. At the end of each day, ask yourself just one question: '**What did I do today to contribute to turning those answers into reality?**'

"Energy and persistence alter all things."

Benjamin Franklin

Chapter 15

Live for now

"Realize deeply that the present moment
is all you ever have."

Eckhart Tolle

Many of us live such highly charged emotional lives with such emphasis and focus on the past and the future that we often forget to just acknowledge the moment we are in. When you are living life 'on the wheel' you tend to have a complete disregard for the here and now, and in fact many of us are actually oblivious to what and how we are thinking or feeling during any given moment during the day.

It's called living on autopilot and it's the result of living unconsciously. Living unconsciously simply means we are living by habit. It is often said that we are 'creatures of habit' and that is such a true statement because if you were to stand back and look at what you did, thought and said yesterday, the likelihood is you will find it was all pretty similar to the day before, that is of course assuming you had some recall of yesterday's events. Even more importantly, if you stop for a moment to think about yesterday and ask yourself what you were feeling and experiencing at various points throughout the day, most of us would not have the first idea. It's just something we did, we got through it, we don't even remember half of the stuff we said and have little or no recall of anything we felt.

You don't even have to go as far back as yesterday, just go back one hour and think about how you were feeling then and what was going through your mind. For many of us even an hour ago might as well be a lifetime ago because we are clueless. We are clueless largely because we are living unconsciously and don't fully understand the critical importance of acknowledging what we are thinking and feeling at any given moment in time and how those thoughts and feelings are directing our lives. I don't mean monitoring each and every thought because that would only drive us completely crazy. No, what I mean is, if you are having a conversation with someone, really be in the moment.

Listen very carefully to what they have to say, rather than waiting patiently for them to finish so you can have your turn and speak. Often we are so focused on waiting to speak we get busy rehearsing what we are going to say and don't fully hear or understand what the person is telling us. What I mean is tasting every mouthful of your meal when you are eating, rather than just shovelling it down like fuel or talking your way through each mouthful oblivious to what you are putting in your body. What I mean is being still for a few moments each day and asking yourself what you are feeling in that very moment. What I mean is not waiting for something to happen or for someone to say or do something before you choose to feel good. What I mean is acknowledging your environment and being grateful and intrigued for the imagination that went into creating it.

To give yourself the brilliant gift of living in the present you need to be aware of what is happening to you, what you are doing and what you are feeling and thinking each moment. It means not judging what you are experiencing now by past events. It's looking consciously at what is happening now, so that you see things as they are now; you are not influenced by fears, anger, desires or attachments.

Take some time out each day, just a few minutes to watch the thoughts that flow through your mind. Are you trying to relive the past? Are you analysing something you did or something that happened to you in the past? Are you thinking how it would have been if you acted differently?

Living in the present means concentrating on what is happening now, enjoying it and making the most of it. If you have been living in the past you now need to think about all the opportunities that you are missing while you are looking behind you. The opportunities are out there waiting to be found and enjoyed. You are never going to find them by looking behind you all of the time or projecting yourself way out in to the future either. You have to be awake to the moment, to NOW.

The challenge is to leave the past behind you and to wake up to the moment and live in it. After all, the past is history; it's gone, so why keep reliving it. What useful purpose does it possibly serve you to keep playing that old movie over and over again. If it's not a pleasant movie, let it go. Even if it's a brilliant movie, don't keep playing it, move on and make a new one. Most of us are so unaware of the process of thinking that's going on in our minds at any given time, that we repeat the same thoughts over and over again purely as a matter of habit. They come and we do nothing to fight or resist them or push them away. In fact we even go as far as to entertain them, regardless of how unpleasant they are. They are just something we seem to get used to; they are just there, a part of us, who we are. As we get used to them they get stronger and stronger, but by becoming aware of them, disputing and challenging them it gradually becomes easier to become a little more detached.

Living in the present means concentrating on what you are doing each moment

Concentrating on the present moment, on what is happening or what you are doing right now, frees you of unnecessary, troublesome and unpleasant thoughts, giving you peace of mind and balance. Think about all of those times you were at the cinema watching a great film, or sitting reading a book that you just couldn't put down or doing something else that you really, really enjoy. Do you recall in those moments thinking about the bills you had to pay or a deadline you had to meet tomorrow, or what your boss said to you a month ago? I would put money on the fact that you didn't think about any of that stuff because you were too busy enjoying the moment. That's the beauty of the moment and there are many more each day and all you need to do is to become aware of them and focus your attention on more of them, nothing else, just moments.

Living in the present develops a whole new kind of awareness and consciousness where you become aware of your freedom, of being alive, of happiness, joy and peace. Just as living in the past can be harmful, always living in the future without appreciating the present is just as damaging. Remember the past has gone and the future hasn't happened yet so don't dwell on either. Create your vision, set your goals and then experience and enjoy each one. What's the point in just waiting to enjoy the goal, because as soon as you achieve it you move on straight to the next goal? Many people waste their time endlessly concerning themselves over the past and daydreaming about the future, and in the process all they do is miss the present.

The present is here with you now, while the same cannot be said about the future. Despite your best planning and intentions anything can happen in the future and you may not even be here very long. Even if you continue to be alive, you may not be healthy in the future. Make the most of now and live the moment, because that is all you really ever have, nothing else, just each moment.

Take your time to understand you...I mean really understand you!

What do you understand about: who you are, what you are made of, where you came from, why you are here, where you are going and why you are going there, who is helping you and who is hindering you, what your values are, what makes you tick, what makes you truly happy, what you are feeling at any given moment, what the possibilities and opportunities are for you in this world, what you want and why you want it, how the universe works and your place in it. These are typical questions that many people go through life paying little, if any, attention to with little understanding of life itself. Without a true understanding of life we have little control of our lives or the future. That's why so many people squander time and end up 'tiptoeing through life hoping to make it safely to death'.

In the absence of asking ourselves some of these questions from time to time and taking time out to understand our own answers, we just react blindly to the world we live in. Doing anything without understanding is like being a paper bag blowing in the wind, just going wherever the wind takes you. Understanding is what separates us from the animal world and the bliss of ignorance is not particularly helpful when you are looking to lead the most fulfilling life possible. I've often heard people say that 'life isn't supposed to be easy' and many years ago that was a term I subscribed to myself, before I realised it wasn't really true. You see, it's my belief that life was meant to be easy but can only be so if you understand it, if you take the time for self reflection and understand who you are and where you are heading. Ignorance is definitely not bliss, as a lack of thought and understanding only leads to a lack of control and balance. If you want to live completely irresponsibly without regard or respect for yourself or others, then I guess that can be termed as easy also, although it's not the kind of easy I would recommend for anyone.

Knowledge and understanding are two entirely different things. You can have a head full of information and knowledge, but it doesn't mean you understand any of it. I have often said, and still believe, that the only way you can truly say you can understand something is when you can explain it fully and properly to someone else so that it makes sense whether they agree with it or not.

Knowing something on an intellectual level is useful if you understand it but knowing and understanding something on an emotional level is what causes you to behave positively. It is said that there are three kinds of people in the world: those who make things happen; those who watch things happen; and those who never know what's hit them. Those who cannot be bothered to try to understand themselves make up the last two categories and are now the great majority of the world's people.

To live your best possible life you need to understand the following three things about yourself:

1. **Where you are** – This means looking at every area of your life and not glossing over anything or denying anything.

2. **Where you want to be** – This is really your vision for your life. How clear is it? How detailed? Does it fit with your life purpose? How badly do you want it?

3. **What price are you willing to pay to get it?** – Understand what it will take for you to be perfectly happy and fulfilled, understand what's in your way

and understand what you are willing to sacrifice to achieve it.

And of course there is just good old time itself!

Have you ever looked in the mirror or reflected on your birthday as to where time has gone. We all say things like 'how time flies', 'I can't believe it's Christmas already', 'where does time go', 'don't the weeks just whiz by'... And it's all true.

At the time of writing this I am 44½ years old and I was having a routine check up with my doctor last week and he reminded me how I need to continue to look after myself 'now that you are approaching 50'. Well, at the time I was mortified, 'approaching 50' was the last thing on my mind. I was a whole 5½ years away from the big five-O and it wasn't something I was ready to think about. When I got home from the doctor and looked in the mirror I kept thinking 50? Where did all that time go? It seems like only yesterday I was still at school, so what happened, where did that time go? It then occurred to me that the doctor was right; 50 was only just around the corner and it would be with me in the very blink of an eye so I needed to be ready.

The point is that life is made up of nothing but time, and when you think about it there really is nothing else, just time, and it's the same for all of us. Regardless of how much money we have in the bank or how nice we are, we all have the same core ingredient of life and nothing else, just time, and it's up to each and everyone of us how we use it. It's an interesting phenomenon that it is the most precious thing in the universe to us humans, yet it is the one thing that many of us take for granted and squander. When we are children and teenagers we convince ourselves that we will live forever and as we become adults we deny our own mortality by thinking about everything else on the planet except how we use time. We act as though we will live forever.

That's all we can do too, use time. We can't do anything else with it just use it and how we use it is entirely up to us. The fact is though, most of us squander time and waste it on things like worry, complaining and generally just drifting through life as though we had all the time in the world. Many of us live our lives in denial that time is finite and it's the most valuable thing a human being can have in this universe, so we need to use it very wisely. Interestingly though, if you consider your own life against the lives of the most successful and fulfilled people who ever lived, you will always find one thing in common. Whoever you consider alongside yourself only ever had 24 hours a day the same as you, not a second more and not a second less, just 24 hours. The difference between the successful and fulfilled and the unsuccessful and unfulfilled is how they use and experience time.

If you choose to spend hours each day in front of the TV then that's your choice; if you choose to engage in work and activities that stimulate you and help you to grow that too is your choice. The point is though that one of the most common complaints you hear in life is how people 'just don't have enough time' or 'there just aren't enough hours in the day to get it all done'.

The reality is that it's not time itself that is the issue, because that is a given, it's constant for all of us no matter who we are, it's how we use time that counts. How we use time depends on our priorities in life. You see, the people who are overweight or unfit because they never exercise their bodies, believe that is the way they are because they don't have time to exercise. The fact is it's just not true; everyone can make time to exercise it's just that some choose not too, it is not a priority.

Just like some people choose to spend every waking hour working, believing they are providing for their family, and then one day their family is no longer with them and they wish they had spent more time with them.

One of the key differences between successful and unsuccessful people is how they see time and how they use it. Time is like anything of value whereby you can use it wisely and effectively, or you can abuse it and waste it. One of the keys to leading a happy and successful life is to use time wisely, to use it to your maximum benefit and advantage.

Ancient Hindu wisdom counsels: 'Look to this day, for it is life, the very life of life. In its brief course lie all the varieties and realities of your existence: the bliss of growth, the glory of action, the splendour of beauty; for yesterday is but a dream and tomorrow is only a vision. But today well lived makes every yesterday a dream of happiness, and every tomorrow a vision of hope. Look well, therefore, to this day! Such is the salutation of the dawn.' (From the Sanskrit)

Here is what you need to do to use time more effectively:

- **Forget time management – manage yourself** – All we can really do is manage ourselves and what we do with the time that we have. Don't try to manage time, manage YOU.

- **Find out where you're wasting time** – Stay away from energy thieves and time wasters. Be honest with yourself and write down where you are wasting too much time: watching TV, using the internet, sleeping, gossiping, phone calls, etc. Ask yourself which of these things are truly contributing to you achieving your goals, being happy, and leading a successful and fulfilled life. Ask yourself where your time could be better spent.

- **Prioritise** – Write down a list of things to do and prioritise them in the order of those things which will add more value to your life in terms of your health, happiness and success. Don't waste time doing things that add no value to you; be ruthless and stop.

- **Don't waste time waiting** – Make sure you have educational CDs in your car so when you are stuck in long traffic jams you can keep on learning. Make sure you carry a small notepad and pen with you so when you are waiting at the dentist, or in a shopping queue you can write down ideas about how to get what you want or how to improve some area of your life.

- **Always stick to the three D's –**

  - **Do it** – don't procrastinate, if it needs doing just do it. Always start the day doing the toughest thing you have to do. You will be amazed at how liberating it feels.

  - **Delegate it** – if it's just not something you should be wasting your time on because it's far more appropriate for someone else to, pass it on quickly.

  - **Dump it** – if something comes your way that just doesn't fit and no one should be wasting time on it then dump it and move on.

Take time for others too!

I once met a man who wore the number two as a badge on the lapel of his jacket and whenever he changed jackets and wore a different one, he transferred the number two badge to the new jacket. He wore the number two all the time, wherever he went.

One day I asked him why he wore the number two and what it meant and I was shocked by his reply: 'I wear the number two to remind me always to put the other guy first,' he said. He then went on to explain that so many people only ever look out for number one (themselves) and he had made a decision a long time ago that he no longer wanted to live like that. Putting the other guy first not only made him feel great but the impact his new philosophy had on others meant that he found that in being more considerate about others that his life became fuller and richer on all levels.

Winning is about making sure everyone wins; it's about making other people feel good as well as yourself. It's about looking for the win/win situation rather than just looking out for yourself regardless of the other person. It is a fabulous philosophy which inevitably leaves you feeling free and enriched as you make a conscious decision to banish the following from your life forever:

- **No more arguments** – Never try to prove someone wrong or yourself right as you always look to see both sides and find the best possible compromise possible.

- **No more dominating** – Stop trying to dominate a relationship either at home or at work. Stop shouting the loudest or trying to get your own way at the expense of someone else.

- **Stop pushing and shoving** to get in front of the queue at all costs, to get a seat on the train or bus when someone clearly needs it more than you.

Winning is about understanding that life is a game but one in which to become a true winner you have to recognise the value and importance of everyone else in the game and treat them with the utmost honour and respect you can. If you charge around the planet just trying to look good all of the time with a complete lack of empathy for others then you never ever get the gold medal. Go out of your way every day to help someone else win either through something you say or do.

It could be as simple as letting another driver on the road come out in front of you or telling someone what a lovely dress or tie they are wearing. It could be holding the door open for someone, smiling at a stranger, buying a homeless person a cup of tea, popping in to check on an elderly neighbour, or phoning a friend or someone you haven't spoken to in a long time to tell them you were just thinking about them. Do something good for charity; either donate clothes or a little money or better still a little of your free time as regularly as you can to give something back.

You see, winning is about recognising and holding as precious the fact that we are incredibly special creatures here on earth and we should be looking out for one another and not going out of our way to score points all the time. When you sit there and complain about your job, give a moments thought to the millions of people unemployed, who would give everything to have your job so they can just put food on the table.

When you are complaining that the fridge is empty and you have to go food shopping, give a moments thought to the millions of people across the world dying of starvation who would love to have the problem of having to go shopping. The next time you find yourself complaining when you are stuck in traffic, just give a moments thought to the millions and millions of very sick people in hospitals across the world who would love to have the health to just drive.

My point is that however little we think we have, most of us actually have so much. Most of us have so much in our own small way that we are already winners and our job as winners is to help others win. It's fine to want more for yourself and to keep dreaming and going for bigger and better goals and becoming an even bigger winner than you already are, as long as part of your plan is to help as many other people as you can win too as well. I believe that without question most of your success and happiness in any single area of your life will come through your relationships with other people, not just those closest to you, but many you have yet to meet. So with this in mind go out of your way to help as many people as you possibly can become winners just like you in the game of life.

These pages contain everything I have learned through research, study and application on my journey through life so far, but particularly over the last nine years since my first encounter with our little furry friend, Botley the hamster. Everything I have shared with you I believe in and have practised and continue to practise and will continue to do so as long as my journey goes on. Botley ran his 15 miles every day and nothing ever changed for him. He taught me that it didn't have to be that way for me and that it doesn't have to be that way for any of us.

We have the one thing that no one can ever take away from us and that is our freedom. No matter how difficult life becomes we always retain that freedom and if we use the myriad of precious gifts bestowed on us at birth, if we can just work out how to use our own manual we can have whatever we want. Nothing is out of reach and the only thing at all which limits us, is us, no one or nothing else on the planet, just us. We don't have to keep spinning endlessly and aimlessly on the wheel to wake up old and tired and wonder what happened and why we didn't make it, that's for hamsters, it not for you and me.

A few short years ago I was exhausted, sick, bored, broke and unhappy with so many areas of my life and the day I stopped my wheel and started to apply all of the principles I share in this book everything changed. The principles aren't mine, some of them are timeless, they are just the ideas that I know work. They worked for me and so I believe they can work for you too.

I went from running furiously on my wheel like a hamster to where I am now living a life of harmony. My journey continues as does yours; like you I still have much to learn and much to do and I can't wait. Stopping my wheel (or rather having my hamster stop my wheel) was the best thing that ever happened to me. I sincerely hope that you will stop yours and live the life you were born to live: a life of great happiness, harmony, peace, health, wealth and fulfilment.

"Happiness is when what you think, what you say, and what you do are in harmony"

Mahatma Gandhi

Printed in the United Kingdom by
Lightning Source UK Ltd., Milton Keynes
136912UK00002B/67-249/P